Reap As You Sew
Spirit at Work in Quiltmaking

> Sue,
> Thank you for sharing your passion & expertise with me + my sisters in The Sea Ranch and Gualala area.
> Blessings,
> Chris

Chris Smith
ReapAsYouSew.com
Chris@ReapAsYouSew.com

If you enjoy this book, please encourage others to read it by posting a review online. I welcome your "Spirit at Work" stories and guest blog posts, and I'm happy to be asked about coaching, speaking, live and virtual workshops, and prayer requests!

TOWARD YOUR CREATIVE GREATNESS AND SACRED CALLING →

CHRIS BOERSMA SMITH

Copyright © 2014 Chris Boersma Smith

All rights reserved. No part of this book may be used or reproduced by any means, graphic, electronic, or mechanical, including photocopying, recording, taping or by any information storage retrieval system without the written permission of the publisher except in the case of brief quotations embodied in reviews and social media posts with proper attribution.

In addition to purchases directly from www.ReapAsYouSew.com, this WestBow Press book may be ordered through booksellers or by contacting:

WestBow Press
A Division of Thomas Nelson & Zondervan
1663 Liberty Drive
Bloomington, IN 47403
www.westbowpress.com
1 (866) 928-1240

NASB indicates scripture quotations taken from the New American Standard Bible®, Copyright © 1960, 1962, 1963, 1968, 1971, 1972, 1973, 1975, 1977, 1995 by The Lockman Foundation (www.Lockman.org). Used by permission.

NRSV indicates New Revised Standard Version Bible, copyright 1989, Division of Christian Education of the National Council of the Churches of Christ in the United States of America. Used by permission. All rights reserved.

NIV indicates Scriptures taken from the Holy Bible, New International Version®, NIV®. Copyright © 1973, 1978, 1984, 2011 by Biblica, Inc.™ Used by permission of Zondervan, www.zondervan.com. All rights reserved worldwide. The "NIV" and "New International Version" are trademarks registered in the United States Patent and Trademark Office by Biblica, Inc.™ All rights reserved.

All photographs, unless otherwise indicated, were provided by the author or the quilters whose stories are told in the various chapters, and all such photos are used by permission. All rights reserved. Credit and thanks go to the following:

Ann Beckett
Donna Blum
Hollis Chatelain
Suzan Friedland
Toby Smith
Jane Shaw Stein
Darra Williamson
Liberty Worth

Many of the quilts shown in this book have been exhibited publicly, juried into shows, and won awards, but in the interests of space, not all such accomplishments have been noted. For more information on the quilters' achievements, please see their individual websites or social media sites.

Cover photo: Copyright 2013 by Chris Boersma Smith, *Let Spirit Flow* (detail)

Because of the dynamic nature of the Internet, any web addresses or links contained in this book may have changed since publication and may no longer be valid. The views expressed in this work are solely those of the author and do not necessarily reflect the views of the publisher, and the publisher hereby disclaims any responsibility for them.

ISBN: 978-1-4908-2370-6 (sc)
ISBN: 978-1-4908-3561-7 (e)
Library of Congress Control Number: 2014908624

Printed in the United States of America

WestBow Press rev. date: 07/07/2014

Contents

Preface iv

Introduction: Stillness, Stats, and Spiritual Paths 1

A Beginner Discovers the Surprising Result of Ordinariness 6

Seagulls at Sunset: Inspiration 13

Resurrection: Darra's Breakthrough 19

Hong Oridney: Anxiety Relieved through Quiltmaking 25

Hope for Our World: Hollis's Social Activism 37

Over Zen: Sue's "Only Don't Know" Approach 51

Like Making Pasta: A Mother-Daughter Healing Quilt 61

Striped Dress: Annie's Discoveries about Art and Beauty 71

If She Had Wings: Donna's Imagination 81

Liberty's Timeline Quilt: A Modern Quilter Pours Her Heart Out 89

Earth-Spirit Emissary Wheel: We Saw the Light 96

The Challenge, Some Gifts, and Conclusions 105

About the Author 111

Preface

I think of myself as a coach and spiritual companion for women who want to pursue their creative passions and freely be their authentic selves. I work heart-to-heart with people who want to break through procrastination, resistance, crippling perfectionism, fear, self-sabotage, and overwhelming stress, so that they get to have more fun and joy … while doing the unique work they were created to do. I love doing this through my writing, quilts, creativity coaching, retreats, and Holy Spirit-inspired spiritual coaching. I've learned that the more we own and use our gifts and free our authentic selves, the more our light shines and the more we enjoy the process of living. Creativity is a divine gift and noble passion that manifests itself differently in each person. My creative juices happen to flow best when I'm open to my close companion, the Holy Spirit, and designing or making quilts.

Reap As You Sew: Spirit at Work in Quiltmaking came to me in a dream. Because of my creative blocks, life events, and spiritual unpreparedness, the manuscript remained unfinished for years. Despite decades of blessings, I now see how much emotional energy I wasted striving, seeking, and feeling not good enough, frustrated, resentful, and like I was in dress rehearsal for an unknown future. Once I realized the futility of that, I resumed this book with a fresh outlook.

Do you know the New Testament story of Mary, Martha, and their brother, Lazarus, who lived outside Jerusalem? Lazarus fell ill, and the sisters sent word to their good friend Jesus to come heal him. By the time Jesus got to their home, Lazarus had been in the tomb for days. Both sisters lamented to Jesus that if he'd come sooner, their brother wouldn't have died. Their demeanors, however, were very different. Martha ran out to meet Jesus as he came up the road. Mary waited until he asked for her, and when she saw him, she fell at his feet. A little later Martha was weighed down, playing hostess to Jesus and all the mourners. Martha went to Jesus, where Mary sat listening to him, and Martha asked, "Don't you care that my sister has left me to do the work by myself? Tell her to help me!"

"Martha, Martha," Jesus answered, "you are worried and upset about many things, but only one thing is needed. Mary has chosen what is better, and it will not be taken away from her." (Luke 10:38–42 NIV; Luke 10:38-42 NRSV; John 11:1–32 NIV).

Circa 1655 by Johannes Vermeer
Christ in the House of Martha and Mary

I've been called a classic overachiever—more of a human *doing* than a human *being*, an overworked and preoccupied Martha. I now choose to live with a better balance of my Mary and Martha aspects. My life and my art flow when I give my Mary her listening time! To execute on the inspiration received in quiet, I call upon Martha-like industriousness. I recently took a course called Developing an Unshakeable Mindset of Success, which taught us how to remove unhealthy thinking and transform our minds with sound beliefs.

With that new improved mindset, and a better balance between my Mary and Martha qualities, I'm free of my old compulsions to seek approval, to prove myself worthy of love, or to stay busy to avoid fear or deep truths.

I've lived my adulthood in increments—five years in marketing, five in real estate, five in law school and then a pressure-cooker law firm, five as a stay-at-home mom helping run a family construction project, five as a part-time attorney while my kids were in elementary school, five as a quasi-single at-home mom because my husband was often overseas, five years dealing with family drama, and five years since all that creating a new empty nest, getting trained as a Christian spiritual director, but still floundering in a turbulent sea of busyness until I ended up beached, flat on my back at age 63. Thank God, my body has since been restored. Most importantly, the six months of recovery time ushered in spiritual and emotional healing. That's when this book was resurrected.

More than a decade ago my pastor asked me to teach a six-week course in an art-as-meditation series. I dug up research to support what I already knew from personal experience, namely: that the practice of quiltmaking offers not only a meditative tool but also an effective form of outreach, community-building, and a means of expressing oneself. At the end of the course, I dreamed of combining all that research and experience with the former attorney part of me that loved writing. Trusting the dream as a divine inspiration, I started to gather my stories into a personal memoir. Then I decided to travel to Guatemala for a writers' workshop.

Before the workshop each writer e-mailed the group one memoir that no one had ever critiqued. I chose a quilt story from the family drama period of my life. It had an openly Christian slant, and it turns out I was one of only two Christians in a group of about fifty writers. My story's content and its religious language didn't fly. I took the criticism hard, without considering that these people were not my target audience and their comments weren't a personal affront. I came home with my bubble burst, thinking my dream was no more than a fantasy.

Journaling one morning three weeks later, Spirit told me to learn from the experience and to broaden my scope from a memoir to a collection of stories about quilters of various spiritual beliefs. I broadcast an e-mail to the membership of a quilt guild I'd just joined in an area where we'd just bought a beach house. The subject was "Spiritual Quilters Wanted." The message read, "I'm writing a book about the spirituality of quilting. I already have plenty of stories from Christians. I'd like to interview spiritual quilters with other beliefs."

Many of the quilters who responded are featured in this book, and they've become dear friends. Retired, award-winning, Hollywood screenwriter and quilter Ann Beckett also helped edit many of the chapters. Her invaluable input not only made the stories more compelling; she also probed me with questions that led me to more self-awareness so I got to reap spiritual rewards as I wrote. I'm profoundly grateful for the twists and turns of this journey, for the willingness of all the women featured in this book who let me tell you their stories and show you their quilts, and for the opportunity to share what we've collectively learned about enhancing the connections between quiltmaking and spirituality.

I'm also grateful for encouragement from my friend and fellow quilter, Marie Bostwick. Many years ago when she was writing her first book, we would talk about our families and our writing dreams, and we'd laugh a lot. I'm happy we've maintained our connection even though we now live on opposite coasts. She's become a *New York Times* bestselling author and has a dozen delightful books under her belt, many of them novels spotlighting spiritual quilters.

My mother, Marie Boersma, launched my love of both quiltmaking and spirituality! Via Minneapolis streetcar I accompanied her to fabric stores before I could walk. As a toddler, I stood on the back of her chair, arms draped over her shoulders, watching skilled hands transform beautiful fabrics into elegant women's wear, draperies, and slipcovers. I can't remember not knowing how to operate a sewing machine! She taught me to follow a pattern meticulously when I was seven. I left for my honeymoon wearing the very stylish tailored suit jacket she'd made in 1947 for her own wedding day. My parents also taught me by example the centrality of faith, and my mom rejoiced more than anyone when I rediscovered and fully embraced the faith of my childhood after decades of spiritual wandering. My love for writing, integrity, and joie de vivre I owe to my dad, Burt Boersma, the journalism major and international publishing world enthusiast who's always been a font of encouragement. Eternal thanks go to both.

For the support to live as my true self and pursue creative undertakings, and for providing me with time, peace, and a place at the ocean, along with his healthy home-cooked meals, my immense love and gratitude go to my husband, Toby. To my lovely, creative, spirited and unique daughters, Kacie and Brenna, who inspire me and lead me to new insights about the world and myself as they courageously pursue their own visual and performing arts and creative writing, I thank you and embrace you with my love! To my grandson Elliott, thank you for sharing your imagination and energy with me. And God bless your desire to be an author yourself!

Finally, I express my thanks to the triune God without whom there wouldn't have been the desires of my heart, the dream, the calling, the strength, or the way . . . for all my steps along the spiritual quiltmaking path, including this book.

Introduction: Stillness, Stats, and Spiritual Paths

At 2 p.m. on a winter day, I was still in my pajamas, sewing. Our kids were away at college. I'd been up for hours, but my hair was unwashed, my face au naturel, my feet still in sheepskins. A fire flickered and sunlight flooded my studio. Long-since drained, a thermos my husband had filled with decaf latte sat on the sewing table. I hadn't even ventured into the kitchen for lunch.

Nine years earlier we'd moved to Northern California, and I'd started a large Indian Orange Peel quilt—as of then still unfinished though I'd made many other quilts over the years. Initially I selected fabrics for the Karen Stone pattern with a new friend, thinking her palette was more developed than mine for a quilt to hang over our mantel against a cranberry wall. I didn't trust my own color instincts. The year before at a guild's quilt show I'd overheard two observers questioning why my *Love Boldly* quilt had won a prize, one saying, "Other than the words, there's nothing special about this quilt," and her companion agreeing, "It isn't original or complex. It just has bright colors."

The orange peel quilt made me miss another quilting friend who'd died. I'd made most of it while I was on quilt getaways with her. After she passed, I'd abandoned the project. By the time I resumed work on it that PJ day in 2006, I'd graduated to selecting my own colors and fabrics, trying to add pizzazz to a top that had become too dull to sustain my interest.

Reenlivened, the eight-year-old project was finally nearing completion, and I was having fun with it. I picked up two strips of fabric, 2½" by the 42" width of the cotton. One had a bold cranberry background and sea foam triangles. A cream and tan created an illusion of texture on the other strip. They worked well together, contrasting in value (light to dark) and scale (size of prints). But my eyes darted to a contemporary violet fabric with slender loden curves swirling toward organic orchid-colored shapes interspersed with surprising copper globules. Rich. Unique. Exciting. From a messy pile I unearthed a subtle sage print, the perfect companion to offset the violet. I happily fed that combo into my sewing machine to create the next of the 220 distinct arcs that would comprise my quilt.

Copyright 1996 by Chris Boersma Smith, *Love Boldly* (40" x 56"). Started in an Elly Sienkiewicz hand appliqué class at Camp Watch-a-Patcher, this quilt won First Place—Hand Appliquéd and Machine Quilted (perhaps a tiny category) at the 1996 *Flying Geese Quilt Show*.

As I sewed, I listened to The Byrds sing, "Turn, Turn, Turn," Pete Seeger's song based on Ecclesiastes 3:1 (KJV), which says, "To every thing there is a season, and a time to every purpose under heaven." In our 24-7 world I knew I had serious time management issues. I seemed to spend the wee hours of my nights corresponding, shopping, paying bills, going to the post office online, sometimes even taking a class, and getting e-mail from my husband's Blackberry as he sat on a runway on the other side of the world. With so much on my to-do list, sleep often eluded me. What I wanted was less stress and more times of peace and quiet. That winter day when I was free to do as I wished—to sew in my PJs—seemed like a great but unfortunately rare day.

Chris Boersma Smith

Copyright 2009 by Chris Boersma Smith, *Persistence* (72" x 72") was based on Karen Stone's Indian Orange Peel pattern and was quilted by Ruth Bass. *Art in the Redwoods Fine Arts Exhibit* 2009, Gualala, CA, Third Place-Quilts; *Pacific International Quilt Festival* 2009, Santa Clara, CA.

Having observed over the years that quilting releases my stress, my husband, Toby, often leaves me to sew alone while he reads newspapers in the family room. But that Saturday afternoon he came in to show me two articles about the business world paying attention to stress. He was impressed because the *Wall Street Journal* reported $10 billion annual revenues for US spas and also tried to tally the cost of lost work time because of stress-induced heart disease. We chuckled over Hannah Kate Kinnersley's March 30, 2006 article titled "Searching for a Stress Buster," which looked at a variety of treatments and therapies to squeeze in, ranging from eye contact and laugh therapy to acupuncture and sound healing sessions in which the client listens to music while being rubbed with something like a bean bag.

The second article, "Zen and the Art of Thinking Straight," announced a new book by a psychiatrist who was Toby's former classmate, Edward Hallowell, a.k.a. Ned. "Wow, even the title of Ned's book, *CrazyBusy: Overstretched, Overbooked, and About to Snap—Strategies for Coping in a World Gone ADD*, explains what I often feel," I commented. I dove into the April 3, 2006 *BusinessWeek* article, which summarized Ned's view that if you frequently feel rushed, impatient, distracted, and forgetful, having taken on so much that even good things like friendship can start to feel like a burden, you need coping strategies (*CrazyBusy*, Ballentine 2006). You have little time for creative thought. You need to prioritize and realize that some of your best thoughts come when you're doing nothing. These publications said what I believe—Americans need to revive the forgotten art of downtime.

Some of you are not the least interested in hanging out all day undressed, but I'm not alone in seeing quilting's benefits. According to *Quilters Newsletter's* "Quilting in America™ 2010," the US quilting market exceeds 21 million women; the trend is upward and although the average age of quilters in 2010 was 62, recent years have seen flourishing interest in quilting and crafting among younger women in the new Modern Quilt movement. I believe this dedication to quiltmaking is precisely because we need to slow down, to relax, and to reflect.

For me, quilting is not only creative—in the design process as well as working tactilely with fabrics—but also blissfully slow. It allows me to experience quiet, alone time, God time . . . or timelessness. I quilt in the present. I'm not focused on the clock. My mind often empties of everyday concerns, making space for contemplation and allowing me to enter a different awareness. To be still is a form of prayer. Quilting—especially hand-sewing—is closer to being than doing relative to the go-go-go activity of my life. And, when I'm still working on a quilt in at-home attire at 2 p.m., I really don't care that dishes aren't done, that there's mail in the mailbox, or that a refill's ready at the pharmacy. We can eat leftovers for dinner. My quilting time has present moment sacredness to it.

Before I started quilting, I dabbled in photography and scrapbooking and tried to relax through cooking and even organizing and de-cluttering. Although temporarily satisfying, each activity ended, and I was still uptight. I saw a therapist weekly. In 1995 I stumbled onto quilting by bringing my portable Singer into my daughter's class to help the kids assemble their art-printed-onto-cotton squares into a quilt for a school auction.

I took a class to learn more and soon found that the repetitive sound of a sewing machine and the rhythm of hand-quilting ushered me into a soothing state. I bought fabric and quit therapy!

When something like quiltmaking becomes as popular as it is, it seems there's some mystery at work. I remember once reading Julia Cameron's assertion in *The Artist's Way* (Tarcher/Putnam 1992) that our souls actually need beauty. More than just using this pastime to slow down, through the art of quiltmaking we express what might otherwise be intangible or unseen. And while much work vanishes, quilts become heirlooms.

Here's why I feel that quiltmaking can be a great spiritual path: Spiritual paths require a commitment of time and usually involve a discipline discovered after some trial and error. Just as a wise personal trainer advises that the best exercise for you is one you'll actually do regularly—and that varies among individuals—so the best spiritual discipline is one you'll actually do. Most quilters would like to spend more time quilting than they currently do, but something stops them. When it hit me that quilting time is spiritual time, the concept was freeing!

A church (where I served for years on a pastoral council) examined ten factors its governing body deemed essential to the congregation's spiritual life. It struck me that quilting has a parallel in all ten areas:
- individuals living out their personal faith;
- gathering as one to raise hearts and minds to what is holy;
- learning and then being transformed;
- developing leadership by using the model of service;
- seeing the divine in all persons and fostering a sense of belonging;
- gathering regularly in small communities to share in an intimate atmosphere and encourage growth;
- respecting diversity;
- using everyone's giftedness in gratitude;
- reaching out to the needy; and
- reaching out to foster transformation and unity.

While each woman ultimately walks her individual spiritual journey, neither spirituality nor quilting is best done solely as a lone endeavor. Both benefit from interaction with others in the pursuit of connection with the divine, personal growth or healing, enjoyment of the fruits, and/or contribution to the larger world. Both nourish the soul of the individual and of others.

If you're already a quilter, the ideas in this book will validate and enrich the quiltmaking process as a spiritual discipline for you. Focusing on the connections between spirituality and quilting—and implementing specific steps to enhance that link—can promote greater contemplation and meditation and yield insights, revelation, and healing, as well as more Spirit-inspired creativity. This book may also encourage you to use your quilting gifts or passion for something you're meant to do, maybe for spiritual outreach, inspiration for others, teaching, or social activism. If you're not a quilter yet, perhaps you'll choose to become one after you read this book. Or you may see how the connections explored here—between creative passions and spirituality—could relate to some other creative art you enjoy, such as needlework or painting.

This book isn't written just for Christians, and only a few points rely on scriptural references. The term *Spirit* is used precisely because some readers and some of the quilters featured in this book don't relate to the term *Holy Spirit*, but all consider themselves spiritual. By capitalizing *Spirit*, I personally mean the most holy spirit, the Spirit of God, rather than the human spirit or any unclean spirit – that is, divine Spirit that can be at work in people or situations whether those involved are Christians or not, but please, read the term *Spirit* as you wish.

If you're not so sure about believing in God or Spirit or trusting the Universe to provide all that's needed in life, please try to suspend doubts for a little while—or turn doubt's volume button from 8 to 7 as you read these real life stories that show Spirit alive and at work—or we might say *at play*. These stories of struggle, breakthrough, realizations, beginnings, healing, and growth show how quilters of different beliefs have found solace and joy through their quiltmaking. There are photos of simple quilts by beginners, masterpieces by professional textile artists, and lots in between. Ideas to consider and manageable steps are presented—some mental, some on paper, some with fabric and thread. You'll probably relate to some stories, reflections, and steps more than others. All are offered with the hope of helping you reap spiritual rewards as you sew.

--- STEPS ALONG A SPIRITUAL QUILTMAKING PATH ---

CONSIDER WHAT A GREAT QUILTING DAY LOOKS LIKE FOR YOU.

ASK AND JOURNAL:
- Where would you be?
- Would anyone be with you?
- How would you dress, eat, and deal with the phone or other interruptions?
- Would you be listening to music, radio, TV, or an audio file, or would you enjoy silence?
- When and how might you create the opportunity for your next day like that?
- What would make it easier?

Throughout this book, where I suggest you CONSIDER or ASK, you may wish to ask the question repeatedly, which gives your brain incentive to explore until it comes up with a good response. The subconscious brain likes to help that way, and so does Spirit. You might even make a small quilted pouch into which you can insert the question you're asking your brain to sleep on—what Laurie Hawley of Aha Life Design calls a "Question Keeper." Read the question before each bedtime, slip it under your pillow, and when you awaken journal what comes up.

READ:
I suggest that you read the short and insightful book *One Small Step Can Change Your Life: The Kaizen Way* by Robert Mauer, Ph.D. (Workman Publishing, 2004). He explains how the subconscious brain responds to repeated small questions, and it will convince you to ask them!

***

CONSIDER WHETHER QUILTMAKING RELIEVES STRESS FOR YOU.

ASK & JOURNAL:
- Is your setup ergonomic so a day spent quilting doesn't hurt you physically? Is the light adequate to avoid eyestrain?
- What do you enjoy about the design and quiltmaking process? How about making a list and referring to it often?
- If quilting is stressful for you, are you focused on the resulting product rather than on the creative process?
- Are there any aspects you don't enjoy? If so, how could you make them more fun? Might there be an easier way to get that part of the process done? Can you break that part down into smaller steps and intersperse them with the more enjoyable parts of the process? Or could you delegate or eliminate that part of the process?
- Are you working on UFOs that no longer really captivate you? If so, can you let them go?

CONSIDER WHAT KEEPS YOU INTERESTED IN QUILTING.
Some possibilities include: satisfying your inner artist, relaxation, friendship and camaraderie with other creative people, expression of things that can't be articulated, outreach, showing compassion, social or political commentary or activism, evangelization or expression of spiritual ideals, teaching about a particular subject dear to you, giving special gifts, and/or providing financial support.

A Beginner Discovers the Surprising Result of Ordinariness

Before I removed my suit jacket, my daughter Kacie came rushing into the entry, grabbed my briefcase, and stuck it in the closet. We hugged and walked toward the kitchen. Conchise was covering the enchiladas, which she made every Wednesday afternoon, the only weekday when I didn't dash out of my office to pull into the carpool line by 3:10. Kacie handed me my purse. "Mom, pay Conchise." The minute Conchise was out the door, Kacie began her pitch as her little sister Brenna watched, silent as a statue.

She announced that she *had* to get her ears pierced because she was the only girl in fourth grade without pierced ears. I hesitated before I responded. I remembered how I longed for pierced ears as a teen, but I thought, *Oh, no, her father (like mine) will have a fit if I let her do this so young.* Rather than speaking from the heart and sharing my own memories and concerns but instead trying to empathize and promote meaningful dialogue, I used the paraphrase technique. "Oh, in your group of friends you're feeling left out without earrings," I said. Both daughters raised their eyebrows and told me I'd obviously been reading parenting books again. They were right. That night I told my husband, "It's scary. The kids are so astute. They always know when I'm trying too hard."

If those 1993 days of my life were seen as cartoons, the archetypal female warrior would stride in one door in pinstriped courtroom attire and emerge on the other side moments later as the archetypal caregiver in worn jeans and a soft pink fleece. But she'd have the same motto across her chest in both costumes, and it would read, "Do It Right." The theme song would be "All for the Cause." Fight for the client, nurture the children.

Next a split scene would show the two characters, each in her milieu and a tug-of-war between them. At work as a lawyer, my white-caped warrior self would wave her sword of words and joust to convince the black-robed judge on his high bench. At home my caregiver self would home-cook meals, read story after story, take the girls to gymnastics, kiss boo-boos, and utter praise every minute or two. Sometimes the warrior would get most of the rope on her side, dragging the caregiver far from the children. Other times the caregiver would tug with all her might, but then after a while she'd only hold onto the rope with one hand, helping other people with the other, dividing her energy until she would fall down exhausted and the rope would slip through her fingers.

Far more than I desired success as a lawyer, I longed for my young daughters to know how much I cared. In an attempt to do parenting right, I strove to fulfill expectations of what would make me a stellar mom, confining myself to a path laid out by others. I'd assimilated those expectations and absorbed the idea that there was a right path—from my parents, I suppose, as well as my 1950s upbringing and the prevalent 1980s and 1990s overachiever and self-esteem-building mentalities.

Looking Back I See My Quilts Sometimes Spoke for Me

When my active parenting days were over, I finally had time to look back and see my strengths and weaknesses, and I realized that they were often the same qualities. Fifteen years after the ear-piercing incident—yes, we'd let her get them pierced—I was sitting in my easy chair, nursing a cold with only my dog for company and a fifteen-year-old quilt tucked around me. *It's strange*, I thought, *how this quilt feels so soft, is so traditional in color and design, and is so unlike me.* And yet memories were all over that quilt like germs. Studying the old quilt, I acknowledged to myself that I'd done my best as a mom, which wasn't even close to perfect, and I'd habitually criticized myself. Obviously I didn't always know what to say. Sometimes I just let my quilts be my voice.

I couldn't forget this quilt's story. When cyberspace grabbed me, I'd just completed five quilts in my first five months of quilting. As a novice, I lacked friends who shared my interest in the craft.

Quilt guilds and friendship groups weren't on my radar yet. I had to find a way of connecting. Showing my dad the newest thing—chat groups and message boards on the new World Wide Web—I stumbled upon a group of quilters who ran *swaps*. Though I later found message boards too impersonal and online swaps too haphazard, my immediate illusion was that this Internet community would offer me collaboration, advice, and enrichment.

For online block swaps, a coordinator would post the theme and rules and act as the clearinghouse. Others signed up and made multiple identical blocks, kept one, and mailed the rest to the coordinator along with a return envelope. After the deadline the coordinator divvied up the blocks and mailed each participant one block from each other participant.

My first swap involved nine-patch blocks made with Debbie Mumm fabric. If I'd known what a Debbie Mumm fabric was, I probably wouldn't have signed up because I favor contemporary designs and bright colors, not traditional small prints in country shades. Clueless, I enrolled, bought Debbie Mumm fabrics, produced multiple blocks, and mailed them off. When the package of nine-patches arrived, my daughters and I tore it open and laid out all the blocks on the living room carpet.

"These don't go together," I moaned. "Look at the points. They don't even match."

"Well, Mom," said Kacie, a budding artist, "maybe you could make two quilts—one with these red and green blocks and another with the brownish ones. But are you going to put all these prints together— seeds and coffee mugs and crows carrying flags too?"

"And watering cans and chickens," piped in Brenna.

"And cats and patchwork and moons in Ohio Stars and checkerboards," I added, laughing at the absurdity of the swap. Until then I'd always sewn perfectly matched clothes, and I'd made a few color-coordinated quilts. My warrior self vowed that I'd be the coordinator for the next online block swap, so I'd control the rules and the selection of which blocks to keep.

Hoping to salvage something from my efforts, I looked up settings in Fons and Porter's *Quilter's Complete Guide*. I decided to follow a diagram that alternated nine-patch blocks and triangles in contrasting colors to form a Straight Furrow setting, creating what looked like diagonal stripes. I attached forest green triangles to the green and red nine-patches, and gold triangles to the brown, black, and gold nine-patches, and then I added borders and corner posts. Looking it over now, I see that the blocks weren't truly a hodgepodge since all the fabrics were from a single designer's line. The prints are small enough that they blended into a cozy quilt much like a grandmother might have made long ago.

Despite thinking I was wasting my time on something that would live in an attic—unloved and unused—I decided (like a good girl) to finish what I'd started. Since this ugly thing didn't merit the time hand-quilting would require, I took a class to learn how to machine quilt. I discovered that the tension on my old portable Singer was unsuitable for machine quilting. At the teacher's suggestion, midway through the project I went to a county fair and test-drove top-of-the-line sewing machines. I took the plunge and finished the quilt on my fancy new acquisition, which I affectionately named "Sophie Bernina." Accordingly I named the quilt "2-M Swap" because it began with a block swap and ended with a machine swap. However, the name didn't stick.

An Ordinary Quilt Takes on a Special Role

Brenna had started to make a name for herself at our neighborhood pool as much as a kid on the 6 & Unders can. That summer she was spending every day at the pool, which was a hundred yards from home. And then in mid-July just as I finished the quilt, she came down with mononucleosis and had to stop swimming. She was couched and needed Mom's TLC.

"Mommy, I feel so bad. I can't even sit up. I'm too tired. I don't feel like eating. And," she wailed, "I'm going to miss practice for days and days and days. I won't get to set any new records the whole rest of the summer."

I pulled out my new 2-M Swap quilt. Tucking it around her shivering little body, I said, "Here, sweetie. This will take the chill off. And since it has my fingerprints all over every inch of it, it's like I'm holding you, even when I can't sit right here with you."

Ever since, my family has called the quilt *The Sick Quilt*. No one has ever had an illness or serious injury in our family without someone—usually one of the kids—going to get that simple patchwork quilt. If you're under the weather, you're under that quilt. A few boring blocks showed me how quilting opened me to the everyday sacred and helped me express compassion in the form of motherly love. Years later when the girls were home from college, we had to evacuate when a fire was encircling our block. With only a few minutes to grab and go, my husband gathered up the photo albums, and I grabbed our dog and my Bible. But the first thing Kacie and Brenna bundled into the car was *The Sick Quilt*.

The Sick Quilt (42" x 53") doing its job a generation later

Allowing Trumps Forcing, and Engaging Trumps Being Right

Still sitting there under *The Sick Quilt* in my empty nest, I thought of the story of Abraham, who lies at the beginning of Judaism, Christianity, and Islam. This nomadic forefather made an unusual and potentially dangerous decision—going out of his tent to greet strangers. Yet, in doing so, he ended up entertaining the divine (angels or messengers) and hearing God's promise. The story shows how reaching out in fellowship and compassion can lead us into the presence of the holy and help us discover our purpose. The key for Abraham was not righteousness and doctrinal certainty, but rather, meeting the needs of others.

My straining to follow the latest theories on what makes a good parent was the parenting equivalent of righteousness and doctrinal certainty. I was trying to follow formulae to achieve correct results—just as I wanted perfect points and matched fabrics to create a masterpiece quilt. Given something I judged inferior—be it mismatched blocks or a lack of a natural gift for parenting from the heart—I needed to learn to work with what was there and set aside my driven idealism. I truly cared about giving my all, but too often I unconsciously swapped intellect-based striving for heart-based living.

Eventually by persevering through doubts and criticism, I've ended up content, not by forcing but by allowing. This principle is reinforced in Psalm 46:10 (NRSV), "Be still and know that I am God!" In other words, stop trying so hard. After loosening up, the process unfolds, and divine inspiration has room to work. The New Testament supports this notion in 2 Corinthians 3:17 (NRSV), which says that where the Spirit is, there's freedom. In other words, when I let go of constantly striving to do right in a universe I saw in black and white, a Spirit beyond my ego freed me through quilting to accept shadows of gray and to live in a world more colored with love.

After *The Sick Quilt* my next few quilts were all made as gifts for cherished friends and family members. I gave away more than half of the hundred quilts I made during the next dozen years. I designed most for the needs, interests, and tastes of the recipients to help them welcome a child, mourn a passing, celebrate a holiday or wedding, or decorate a new home. Quilts became a way for me to express what was difficult to say with words. Many of the simple quilts I made as a beginner still grace the homes of the recipients, not only showing them I loved them when I made the quilts but continuing to remind people of my care as time goes on. Touching down where I have walked along life's path, those quilts are my rainbows.

--- STEPS ALONG A SPIRITUAL QUILTMAKING PATH ---

NOTE: The spiritual aspects of quilting are not One Size Fits All. The suggestions in these sections at the end of each chapter are what I've experienced, observed, or heard from quilters I've known or interviewed. You might try whichever ones resonate with you first. Later, you may come back and try others. Diversity is a natural part of intentionally quilting with openness to Spirit.

CONSIDER CREATING AND/OR MAINTAINING YOUR OWN PHYSICAL ALBUM OR ELECTRONIC QUILT DOCUMENTATION SYSTEM.

REMINDER: To avoid feeling overwhelmed, create your documentation records in small steps. Just start with the photos that are easiest to find, or simply implement a good system going forward!

ACT: If you don't already have one, select an album style or electronic library or file system that allows you to re-order and add pages or files later.

TO CREATE QUILT DOCUMENTATION, FOR EACH QUILT, INCLUDE:
- Photos—at least a full photo of the front; an optional one of the back, close-ups to show quilting or more detail, and a picture of the quilt where it now lives
- the name of the quilt and perhaps the meaning of the quilt's name
- the dates it was started and finished and perhaps where you were when you made it
- its size
- whatever it says on the label (if not legible in a photo)
- Information about whether the quilt was appraised, sold, donated to charity, exhibited, or won any awards as well as any artist's statement you submitted.

You may also wish to include:
- what inspired it
- what techniques and batting were used
- scraps or scanned in images of dominant fabrics in order to record their true color or texture

A PARAMOUNT RECORD TO INCLUDE IS WHAT LESSON OR LESSONS YOU LEARNED FROM EACH QUILT.
- Technical—Some quilts teach lessons on technique. (For example, if metallic threads keep breaking, change the needle and don't assume the new needle is burr-free because it may take more than one new needle to solve the problem.)
- Practical or design-related—Sometimes you learn about buying fabric in certain quantities or solving design challenges. (For example, maybe you noticed the effect of mixing large-scale prints with smaller-scale geometrics and directional fabrics.)
- Spiritual, philosophical, or psychological—Lessons may be about life or God or people or yourself. (For example, I learned that I can't do a huge project like a memory quilt with blocks contributed by all a couple's family and friends and then attend their wedding or anniversary party as anything other than "the quilt lady.")
- Self-discovery—Working on the quilt or presenting it to others may have revealed some point of self-awareness. (For example, I learned I can't make myself work on a big unfinished project out of a feeling of obligation. I can only make progress when I let go of the idea of obligation, substitute an

idea of blessing, and/or proceed by honoring my desires and instincts, and taking one small step and then another.)

42" x 53"

"2-M Swap"

This quilt was made with Debbie Mumm fabric 9-patches swapped through America Online, hosted by Karen Cummins (ANURS) of Davenport, Iowa. I made my red strawberries and green blocks around May 27, 1995. The exchange was sent back around June 15, 1995. When I got the blocks, I played with them, first thinking no coordination was possible. Then I found the Straight Furrows layout in the Fons & Porter Quilter's Complete Guide, made two extra blocks, the corner, and set the blocks in the green and gold Mumm fabrics, which cost $6.95/yd. at Piecemakers.

I feel that this quilt challenged me to come up with something I never would have done on my own, both in color and layout, and I like the effect. The quilting was a nightmare when I began it on my Singer, trying both the walking foot and free motion quilting in the ditch, but getting puckers either way. Because of this, I decided that I truly needed a new machine, so in the middle of the project, I bought a Bernina 1260 and finished quilting on that. What a difference! The quilt was finished July 19, 1995.

This quilt is so soft that we curl up in it to comfort us as our family's "sick quilt."

Name explanation: Mumm block swap quilt & machine swap.
Blocks were made by these online friends:
Judy Richards (Nysepstcht) Cranbury, NJ; Jgraham826; JoniRN, Davenport, Ia; Angela Wentworth (Sewquilter) Exeter, RI; Eunice Graff (EuniceGraf); Donahue, IA; Rose Gray, Pinkerton, OH; Shelley Kuncio (GRAMA) Boston, MA; Karla Denton, Topeka, KS; Karen Galley (Galikon31) Lawrenceville, NJ; Donna Sheffer (Dsheffer) York, PA; An Unknown; Karen Cummins (ANURS) Davenport, IA, and me (Chrickie B) Newport Beach, CA.

Sample physical quilt album

CHIHULY REFLECTIONS
Copyright 2013 by Chris Boersma Smith
The Sea Ranch, CA 95497

37" x 29"

Story: I started this quilt after doing a series of drawing exercises in a Hollis Chatelain Masters Series class. Thinking about luminosity, transparency, and reflected light, I was drawn to some pieces of colored glass, which I tried unsuccessfully to set up for an exciting still life. Then I started looking online at images of the work of Dale Chihuly, whose glass sculptures I'd admired in Naples, Florida and at the De Young Museum in San Francisco, and I based my design on a small portion of one of his large installations. I worked on this piece over eleven months, often thinking of the Light of the world, sometimes asking Spirit to help me with thread selections, and approaching the quilting in a completely new way for me, from background to foreground, leaving my favorite parts for last. As it neared completion, I got out my sea sponges and dabbed on some painted highlights to enhance the thread highlights. It's a process-oriented quilt that was a lot of fun to execute and I believe it incorporates a spark of spirit. It hangs in my seaside dining room, where some interpret it as an underwater scene.

Lessons: Amidst the quicker projects, I like to put extra effort into some pieces like this one. Saving a focal point to quilt last worked well, and I think quilting bubbles is something I'll do often. It took courage to sponge on paint near the end but it really added to the overall effect.

Sample digital portfolio page

OBSERVE:
- Once you've documented your work, take time to read through your album or digital pages. Notice or pray for awareness in identifying any themes to your quiltmaking as well as any tendencies, growth, or lessons that keep appearing.
- You may choose to tally how many quilts you've made over the years, how many you've kept, and how many you've sold, donated, or given away. You may be surprised.

CONSIDER YOUR GIFT QUILTS:
- Review to whom you've given quilts, what motivated you, and how the recipients responded. Were there lessons?
- How much do you use your quilts to say something special, to make your love or compassion visible?
- What valuable insights did your review and evaluation provide for you? Which quilts or which type of quilts brought you the most joy or satisfaction?

DECIDE: As a result of this review, will you set an intention to do some kind of quilting more or less often, more discerningly, and in greater quantity but smaller sizes, or make fewer but larger pieces?

SHARE: I'd love to have you e-mail chris@reapasyousew.com and tell me about what you learned from reviewing your past quilts.

Seagulls at Sunset: Inspiration

When *The Artists' Way* came out in 1992, I worked through every page of that seminal book on creativity. I began author Julia Cameron's recommended practice of writing "Morning Pages," and I've journalled ever since. She also urged artists—whether quilters, writers, painters, or anything else creative—to set aside time every week to do something fun all by yourself in order to get away from the shoulds and the busyness, enjoy your own company, and get a little inspiration. I pursued that practice for a while but somehow for me these so-called "Artist's Dates" became my margin-for-error time. I squeezed in every unpredictable activity by breaking dates with myself. Though understandable that this might occur occasionally, the pity was that it happened so frequently that I soon forgot about the whole concept. My creativity became limited by e-mail and bills, saying yes to volunteering when I wanted to say no, not letting go of UFOs (unfinished objects) that no longer held my interest, and pursuing competing hobbies like scrapbooking, decorating, cooking, and writing. Inspiration waned. Quilting productivity dropped, and deep longing was not getting its due expression, which is why I felt called to attend a 2006 *Artists' Way* for Quilters workshop.

I'd taught spirituality of quilting classes in 2001 and had already written parts of this book when I heard of the workshop. Unfortunately the workshop was full. But I contacted the organizer the same day someone broke her foot and canceled, and I got her spot.

Even before the workshop began, overcommitment was robbing me of artistic enjoyment. Before I left for the drive to Asilomar, I attended a three-hour meeting for a church council I'd been on for three and a half years, a volunteer

Photo Courtesy of Aramark and Asilomar Conference Grounds, Pacific Grove, CA

Chris Boersma Smith

Photo Courtesy of Aramark and Asilomar Conference Grounds, Pacific Grove, CA

position requiring hours per month of preparation time. We were trying to complete a strategic plan that had begun years earlier with research, surveys, and interviews. The meeting had been a disaster. The worst example of something written by committee was going to emerge. I spent the several-hour drive trying to calm down, and I might have foreseen that I'd have sleepless nights over this at Asilomar. Experiences like these were all too common in my life.

This was the first time *The Artists' Way* for Quilters was taught at Asilomar, a beachside conference center amidst the pines in Pacific Grove, California. Like me, many of the participants had gotten an *Artists' Way* shot in the arm years earlier but were now here for a booster. Cartoonist Earl Storm, our certified *Artists' Way* instructor, wore a garish Hawaiian shirt with a shirttail down to the back of his knees. I immediately pegged him as a free-spirited drama queen (which he later admitted). I knew I was supposed to be there.

Day 1: The Artist's Date

The first morning we got to experience childlike creativity with a series of playful fabric-painting exercises. After lunch Earl sent us off on solo Artist's Dates, and quilting instructor Alex Anderson suggested that we notice things that evoke strong sensations or emotions, write down a few words on an index card, and/or take a digital photo to help us recall what impresses us.

On my car's out-of-date navigator I keyed in, "Tourist attractions, sorted by distance." What attracted me most was a historic house on a street called Ocean View, so that's where I went. On the way I passed a simple, steepled white church built in 1895, with Victorian art glass. It sat on a corner with its back to the ocean four blocks downhill. I stopped and took a picture of the church with the backdrop of the ocean, got out an index card, and wrote, "Spirituality and the sea—such a connection." Back in my car I continued following the navigator. As I pulled up to the programmed location, all I found was a neglected, turn-of-the-century house hidden behind massively overgrown trees that blocked a view of Monterey Bay. I took some photos and thought about how I'd love to remodel that place!

I parked and crossed the street to a grassy knoll overlooking a bluff trail. It was after five o'clock, and the path was dotted with walkers and their dogs. I captured digital images of them, got out another index card, and wrote, "The faithfulness and loyalty of dogs—unconditional love."

I savored the salt air, and then I heard them—seagulls at sunset. Suddenly I was transported back thirty years to my house abutting the sandy shore of Long Island Sound. I remembered waking up to the birds' good morning calls and then listening to the trickling of the water through rivulets in the cove if it was a week of low tide at dawn or hearing the crashing of waves when it was high tide at that hour. I remembered coming home from work and flopping on a lounge chair on the deck as the sun set and the seagulls serenaded me again.

My body felt lighter. Already upbeat after the morning's fabric painting, my mood seemed to match that of the birds. When the air started to cool, I realized it was time to go if I was going to get dinner. It didn't even occur to me to write on an index card.

Day 2: The Quick Concept Quilt Challenge

Alex instructed us, "Get out your index cards and pick the one that captured the strongest concept for you." As much as I loved the image of the church and nearby sea and the photos of dogs and their human companions and despite having no index card or photo of the scene, I selected the seagulls at sunset. "Your challenge," said Alex, "is to create in just three hours a quilt top that will convey aspects of your concept without actually depicting it."

My tendency was to attempt a pictorial landscape, but I knew that wasn't the lesson. How could I not picture the birds and the beach and all I'd visually embraced the afternoon before? I focused as directed on attributes instead of images—ideas of flight, the birds always appearing in multiples, how they make tracks in the sand. I zeroed in on the colors of the birds, sky, water, and dark rocks marked with white bird droppings. I remembered the road and the green knoll between the houses on Ocean View and the curved bay of saltwater. I wanted to use the fabrics I'd painted that morning and realized one had orange shapes like sharp-pointed boomerangs or chevrons. I decided the color was a sunset color, and the shape resembled a gull in flight. Surprisingly that led me to think of a traditional block.

Working fast with only so much fabric and not all the usual drafting supplies, perfectionism was out the window. I still didn't have a clear idea of an overall quilt design, but I started making flying geese blocks in a liberated style—no ruler, no measuring, in different sizes and colors of whites and grays just as the seagulls would differ from one another. I pieced some triangles that reminded me of the water churning and splashing around the rocks. I added some greens to represent the plantings and some geometric gray blocks for the road. I ironed some Wonder-Under to a little black fabric, and then I cut out and pressed on some abstract, illogically sized marks that reminded me of bird prints in the sand. I composed a strata of yellows along with oranges. The parts went together, but they didn't logically follow the layout of a landscape. It was seat-of-the-pants work, right-brained, and fun!

By the end of the allotted time, I'd produced a small top that will always remind me of my love for the beach. It doesn't matter that it's not a masterpiece of design or construction. I'd allowed my feelings rather than my head to direct my work. And the product would speak to me for a long time, not only of seagulls and the tranquility I feel at the beach but also of the importance of Artist's Dates and the recognition and expression of longing.

Copyright 2014 by Chris Boersma Smith, *Seagulls at Sunset* (14" x 16") (finally quilted and finished for this book)

Day 3: Dream Big and Take the Steps That Start to Appear for You

The next morning Earl stressed the importance of active imagination. "Spend time with your hopes and dreams," he advised. "Dream big. Put them in your Morning Pages. Sit with them and see just how you'd like your art, your life to be. Then watch them unfold. You'll see little openings. Take them. Big dreams, then small next steps."

He directed the group to sit for some time in silence. I envisioned a day when my book on the connection between spirituality and quilting would be published and I'd be using that work along with my training in spiritual direction to run workshops for quilters who want to use *quilting as a means to spiritual ends*. ("As you sow [sew], so shall you reap") in addition to the direction we explored in *The Artist's Way* for Quilters, which spoke of *spirituality as a means of achieving artistic goals*. After I allowed my imagination free reign for a while, I slid into my old habit of analyzing—thinking about practicalities, using the present to veto the future. *How would I pay for these dreams? How could I find the time? What if someone else does it better? How would that fit with my husband's job? Maybe I don't have enough talent.*

Then I began to feel what I'd felt the night before. After dinner I'd attended a prayer meeting at the historic Carmel Mission. Singing along with the song "Hold Me Close," I'd initially felt like I was dancing with my father—a fond childhood memory. But then my dance partner seemed to be God the Father or the Lord of the Dance. I sensed that God was physically holding me and loving me, a sensation so real that I became convinced in that moment that God is all I need. I felt so free my heart was like a feather. Remembering that, my inner artist returned to the reverie.

I imagined that women would connect deeply and grow in community. Journal-writing, something like one-on-one coaching, and spiritual direction would be available in addition to opportunities for quilting, painting, or dyeing fabric. I even imagined the perfect place for these workshops—in the remodeled tourist attraction behind the trees. I vividly imagined its inspiring views from every room, plenty of guest rooms with luxurious down comforters and marble baths, a living room and parlor big enough for a workshop, and a beautiful dining room for sharing nourishing meals.

After this musing Earl asked, " What stops you from making the quilts you want to make?"

I love to write, I thought. Lately I'd been writing more than quilting. "Sometimes I feel like a woman with too many hats," I said to Earl at the break. "But can't I be passionate about more than one creative form of expression?"

"Of course," he said.

"What I really want to do is combine them," I explained.

"Do it," he answered.

After the morning session I fell into step with a group trekking to lunch, and we kept discussing what blocked us. I mentioned to one of my classmates my desire to write, quilt, serve as a spiritual director, and combine them all. She smiled and said she understood about writing and quilting competing for your time and creative energy. She told me that years ago she wrote a book titled *Sensational Scrap Quilts*. I shared the idea of my book, forgetting my usual reluctance to share it for fear that someone else might write the same thing first. She encouraged me, and we parted to pick up our lunches. After I sat down, she came to my table and handed me her card, saying, "Call me when you get home." I looked at the card, which read, "Darra Williamson, Editorial Consultant." And her specialty? Working with publishers of quilting books!

Following the lead of my dancing spirit with more grace than ever, the next week not only did I call Darra, but I designed and worked on four quilts, wrote two chapters, and resigned from that aggravating volunteer position.

--- STEPS ALONG A SPIRITUAL QUILTMAKING PATH ---

ACT: If you haven't already read it or if it's been a long time and you wish to revisit it, get *The Artist's Way* and a journal and work your way through the book. If you've already read that book, select a different inspirational book for artists. I keep updated lists of book recommendations on www.ReapAsYouSew.com and on my coaching website, www.Heart-to-Heart.net.

PONDER YOUR DREAMS. Besides regular journaling, pray about your dreams (if you pray), write them in your journal, and start watching for open doors. You may also choose to work through your dreams with a spiritual director or therapist.

CREATE REMINDERS: At *The Artist's Way* for Quilters workshop, we used childlike toys and whimsical objects to remind us of creative objectives. For example, while in Pacific Grove, I found a ceramic model of two bug-eyed green frogs playing leapfrog. The frogs remind me to approach my art with childlike abandon.

- List one or more qualities or approaches you'd like to remember when you're in your studio or work space. Look back at the positive associations you identified in your quiltmaking process when asking and journaling the questions on page 5.
- Jot down words or images that might symbolize each for you.
- Find, buy, or make physical reminders to keep where you'll see them. You could collage images, doodle, draw, or find an object you'll be sure to notice. Or even make a quilt or drawing incorporating these visual reminders.
- Put any reminder objects in your studio or on a Pinterest board to remind you of what you want to embody in your creative approach.
- Alternatively or in addition, create an iTunes playlist that reflects those qualities or approaches, and play it to help get your creative juices flowing.

ACT:
- Give yourself a few hours for an Artist's Date.
- Afterward, note what excited you most.
- Then within the week, give yourself just half a day to make a quick quilt top that suggests the concept or essence of what touched you—not a realistic or precise quilt, just a quick creative challenge.
- If you like what you made, you may quilt it or expand the quick version into a larger or more refined quilt. If you like the process, use it often.

ACT: Plan to go on a quilters' getaway, even if just a weekend, perhaps even at the home of one of your quilting friends when she has her home all to herself. Break your getaway action plan into small steps to make sure you can accomplish it without resistance! Enjoy this special bonding and productivity time! If you can, make it a regular (perhaps annual) event. Or consider signing up for a quilters' retreat organized by someone else, with or without teaching. Many quilt shows offer classes, and retreats are often listed online.

Resurrection: Darra's Breakthrough

Resurrection is a noun referring to the rising of the dead. Synonyms include renaissance, restoration, resurgence, and revitalization. Symbols representing resurrection include a cross, radiating light, depth, earth, and heavens. The effects of these images can encompass comforting, honoring, mourning, connecting, remembering, healing, touching, teaching, transforming, inspiring, or freeing.

How would you feel about applying even half these spiritual words to describe a single quilt that you created? Every one of these powerful descriptors applies to Darra Duffy Williamson's 1994 quilt, *Resurrection*.

Copyright 1994 by Darra Williamson, *Resurrection* (39" x 54"), made in honor of Jean Stever (1930–1982). Photo by Todd Bush, www.bushphoto.com (2014).

Today Darra is a respected professional in the quilting and publishing world, a woman who combines warmth with strength, passion with playfulness, quilting with writing, and living with loving. She is best known for the engaging teaching style that got her named Quilt Teacher of the Year in 1989 by the *Professional Quilter* magazine and as author of *Sensational Scrap Quilts* (AQS, 1992). She was also the editor of *Creative Embellishments* (Rodale Books, 2001). In 2001, she was a guest on HGTV's *Simply Quilts* with Alex Anderson, and from 2001 to 2003, she was the editor-in-chief at C&T Publishing. Since then, she's had fulfilling freelance work as an editorial consultant specializing in quilting books and patterns. She's coauthored with Christine Porter *A Year in the Life of Sunbonnet Sue* (That Patchwork Place, 2010) and *Cuddle Me Quick: 11 Baby Quilt Designs* (That Patchwork Place, 2012), and she participates in a successful blog, which she enjoys doing with three professional quilting friends.

Quiltmaking Filled a Gap in Darra's Life

Looking back, Darra says it's clear that her whole life was preparing her for this career and that *Resurrection* ushered in her personal renaissance. Having studied English and journalism, Darra first taught high school and later worked for a newspaper as a reporter, editor, and instructor (showing teachers and students how to incorporate the newspaper into the classroom). Living in South Carolina, she collected American antiques. After buying antique furniture, she began adding accessories, and that led her to collect antique quilts. One day in her early thirties, she uttered the sentence most quilters say one life-changing day, "Hey, I'm sure I could do that."

She took a beginner's quilting class and called to tell her mother, an accomplished seamstress who'd sewn everything except quilts. Darra's mom guffawed. They were close enough for Darra to take the kidding. Both knew Darra could barely thread the machine and sew a straight line. But she'd been smitten. She felt quilting would enrich her, adding something fun to a life jam-packed with work. In quilting she'd found the missing piece!

Tragically before her first quilt was even finished, Darra got a call that seemed as real as an announcement that Martians had landed on the front lawn. Her dad was on the phone, and by that very fact, she knew it was bad news. At 51, with no prior symptoms or warnings, her mom had awakened feeling unwell, suffered a heart attack, and died. Darra flew to her New Jersey hometown and went through the funeral and what she sees now as superficial grieving.

After about two months she said to herself, "Okay, buck up and get on with it." So she got busy. She finished her first quilt, which she longed to have been able to show to her mother. She made a few more and brazenly started teaching quilting in her home to groups of six. While she knew she couldn't sew as well as her students, her teaching background, the years of collecting and appreciating the geometry of antique quilts, and an innate sense of color gave her something to share that others wanted. After all, it didn't take an expert seamstress to inspire people to explore quiltmaking or to experience greater creativity.

Her husband was supportive of her new interest, and she began teaching up to four quilting classes a week in local and regional shops and continuing education programs in addition to freelance writing. Her dad was also supportive. They'd gotten closer since her mother's passing, and he'd stop in local quilt shops on his travels and buy her fabric.

When she was presented the Quilt Teacher of the Year Award at the *American Quilter's Society Show* in Paducah, Kentucky, in 1989, her quilting career really ramped up. AQS invited her to teach the following year and suggested she write a quilting book. She was catapulted from regional teaching to the national circuit. She was in demand and on the road.

During this time and just two years after she'd lost her mother, Darra lost her husband suddenly. She bought into someone's notion that you're allowed to cry over the loss of a loved one for about two months and that then if you just got back to work, that'd straighten you out. Despite these two huge losses, she just kept going. Quilting was Darra's life and her livelihood. Busyness was her coping mechanism—or rather, her escape and her excuse.

Recent photo of Darra on the Mendocino coast

It Took a Meltdown for Darra to Grieve through Her Quilting

In 1992, ten years after her mom had died, Darra's dad asked her to make a quilt honoring her mother. In retrospect, she thinks her father probably realized that there was a lot she hadn't dealt with and needed to address. He probably thought this might be a way for her to get out what she needed to express. But Darra was afraid that starting to make such a quilt would open the floodgates and that her tears might never stop. Darra had 101 excuses why she couldn't, wouldn't, or didn't want to make a quilt in her mother's honor.

In January 1994, Darra had a major meltdown. Her extreme busyness and her unfinished grieving caught up with her. She'd postponed fully feeling her losses, and here she was—motherless, teaching, writing magazine articles, working on books. And she simply couldn't do it anymore.

She's very open about this period, what used to be called a "nervous breakdown." She wouldn't even enter her quilting room. She cancelled two solidly booked years of teaching engagements. She didn't even answer the phone. At first people thought she had cancer, but eventually many came to know that she'd pushed herself to total burnout.

She was about six months into that dark time, and in the process of therapy she abruptly told herself that making the quilt for her mother would be a therapeutic way to deal with her grief. From the start she set three goals. First she'd create something that would indeed honor her mother. Secondly she wanted to create something appropriate for hanging in a Catholic church, even though she was no longer attending church herself. Her parents were devout Catholics. They'd been very active in their church in New Jersey, and her dad had asked her to make a quilt to donate to that church, the one she'd also grown up in. Thirdly she wanted the quilt to reflect her own personal style.

Darra Emphasizes that She Didn't Design This Quilt Consciously

With that tall order, Spirit came in. Darra went into her sewing room, and fabric just started flying. She hadn't bought any new fabric. She doesn't remember where the idea came from, but she wanted a cross to be the central image. She also knew she wanted the feeling to be hopeful, focused on an image of resurrection rather than memorial or death. She started flipping through her quilt books. She felt drawn to a block that suggested rays of light. That radiating block—called Crown of Thorns (a Christian symbol of Jesus' pain and a mocking of his authority)—became the quilt's central image as Darra roughed out a sketch.

Crown of Thorns block. Photo by Todd Bush, www.bushphoto.com (2014)

Darra's recent quilts had all been scrap quilts so, true to her style, she would use many fabrics. She'd been toying with the then rather new ideas of incorporating color wash or color grading into her work, so she decided this quilt would provide her with that opportunity.

At first the quilt was comprised of squares that went all the way out from the cross motif to make a rectangular top, but in a break from her typical approach, she was moved to try a new technique for her. Cutting away some of that top, she created an arch that she appliquéd onto a different background. Not only was this arch a potent and pleasing image to Darra personally, but its curve also reminded Darra of church imagery. Later she learned that the arch is a symbol of the female.

Photo by Todd Bush, www.bushphoto.com (2014)

"It was amazing," Darra told me. "As I worked on it, it just seemed like I was the instrument. And the quilt, the imagery, the idea was driving the design. I have little recollection of making conscious decisions as to what needed to happen. In fact," she interjected, "it was when we did *The Artist's Way* for Quilters that I remembered that sense of letting go and being the instrument. Even the borders on the quilt . . .." She paused and then continued, "When I got ready for borders, I didn't have enough of the gray fabric I was going to use, so I used two different ones, and that contributed to the quilt's dimension and depth. The quilt just literally evolved."

"When I was done with it—and to this day—I'm still in awe, not because I produced this great work of art, but because I can't believe that what I wanted to say so sincerely came out of me uninhibitedly and unintentionally. It just happened, and it got done very quickly once I started." Even with the hand-quilting (mostly lines radiating out from the center, and a vine with leaves to symbolize rebirth and growth in the borders), the quilt was completed in a month—a month where she felt focused but not under any pressure or compulsion to complete the piece.

Looking at the photo of the quilt during our interview, I saw a monstrance—an open or transparent receptacle in which a consecrated host (believed to be the real presence of Christ) is exposed for veneration in the Catholic tradition. I asked Darra whether she'd seen or intended that to be seen. No, she hadn't planned it. It just revealed itself to her on the design wall.

She began to see different things as she worked, she said, without purposely designing them. She restated emphatically, "What I want to convey is how the creative process was unfolding without my conscious participation. I just started from the center on a design wall and worked out, initially only knowing there was to be a cross and an uplifting feeling." The rest was Spirit at work.

The Finished Quilt Works as a Vehicle for Healing

While working on the quilt, Darra cried with a combination of sadness, release, joy about finally expressing her feelings, as well as astonishment about the process. She felt her mother's presence with her so absolutely that she feels closer to her mother now than she did when her mother was alive, and she'd felt close to her mother as an adult daughter.

Darra had also met her goals of honoring her mother, being true to her own style, and making something suitable for hanging in her hometown's Catholic church. However, since her father had suggested that place for it, the pastor had retired. His replacement didn't know the family, and by then Darra had been estranged from the church for twenty years. During her father's frequent stays with Darra at her home, which was then in Boone, NC, he'd always go to St. Elizabeth.

Her dad would go alone because he'd been telling Darra since she'd stopped going to church in college, "I just have a feeling that when the moment is right, you'll come back." When he saw the finished quilt, he said, "Darra, why don't you take it to St. Elizabeth to see if they'd like to have it because that's such a beautiful setting? It's a place your mother would have loved, and it's become really dear to me."

Darra brought it to show the pastor, and he was delighted to have it. Speaking with him briefly, Darra expressed her reservations frankly, saying she hadn't had a good relationship with the church for quite some time.

"Well, there's no obligation here," he replied, "but this is your home. You're always welcome here. And if you'd like to come and visit the quilt anytime, feel free."

He showed her where the quilt would go, on a river-stone wall. Darra thought the quilt against that rock was just beautiful. She also thought she was finished with this quilt.

Initially installed against a stone wall at St. Elizabeth of the Hill Country and Epiphany Church, Boone, NC, *Resurrection* is shown here next to the sanctuary. Photo by Todd Bush, www.bushphoto.com (2014).

A month later Darra attended a memorial service for a friend's father at the same church. The quilt was hanging there. Gazing at it during the service, she decided to revisit it. The next Sunday she returned, and while she was there, looking at the quilt during Mass, she heard a plea for new choir members just for that Christmas. This is what Darra's sisters call "Mama's first miracle."

Darra ended up singing in the choir beyond Christmas—in fact, for two more years—and then she actually joined the parish. The welcoming community had become a meaningful part of her life. She felt no pressure to buy the whole package, but she found needed comfort and lasting friendships. The singing was prayer for her. She got involved because the community participated in Habitat for Humanity and provided meals for a homeless shelter, and the social justice focus satisfied her.

Five months after she'd completed the quilt and one year into her two years of therapy, Darra finally mustered the courage to show a photograph of *Resurrection* to her therapist. She mentioned that this was her very first quilt with symbolism in it as well as the first time she "just completely winged it." A light flashed on for the therapist, who had no previous idea of what a quilt could be. Looking back, Darra says that first year of therapy was like triage. The second year delved into intense personal work that grew out of the imagery in the quilt and eventually other quilts she shared with him.

Resurrection became a healing vehicle not only for Darra but for many. It helped Darra complete her grieving process for her mother and her husband—well, as complete as it ever gets. It brought her back to a level of faith and spirituality she thought she'd abandoned forever, reawakening a spiritual aspect of her life to this day. And the parish used the quilt during well-attended monthly healing services, where the sick and suffering came for physical, emotional, and spiritual healings. Many who were moved by it would call and tell Darra how the quilt comforted them or lifted their spirits.

The Fringe Benefits of Letting a Quilt Evolve

Finally what Darra learned from spiritually surrendering while working on *Resurrection* was the joy of discovering that a quilter could let go and let a quilt evolve. With that realization, Darra's following years were prolific, and every quilt she made in the next two years sold. "People see something in quilts made like that, whether it's what the maker intended to express or something else. Those quilts tug at people, who then want to have them," she said.

Darra now taps into her true self, her heart, her personal imagery, her dreams, her love of Mendocino, whatever comes to her as spiritual resource material. When Spirit inspires the maker of a quilt, the invisible spark of spirit incorporated into the work also touches viewers.

Copyright 2012 by Darra Williamson, *Bloom* (13.5"x9"). Note the serendipitous similarities between Bloom and Resurrection.

--- STEPS ALONG A SPIRITUAL QUILTMAKING PATH ---

CONSIDER WHETHER YOU'D LIKE TO INTENTIONALLY CREATE A QUILT TO BE DESCRIBED WITH CERTAIN SPIRITUAL WORDS OR OTHER DESIRABLE DESCRIPTORS.

ASK & JOURNAL:
- If you've already made quilts that can be described with such words, good for you! How was your experience similar to or different from Darra's? How about if you sit and feel the feelings again? Have you changed your design process as a result?
- If this would be a new approach for you, jot down the descriptive words you'd like to work with, either in your Morning Pages, art journal, or on a paper you might tack to your design wall-- wherever you'll see the words—and let them inspire you as you unconsciously and/or consciously take them in day after day.
- Look back over quilts you've made. Do any of them incorporate symbolism? If so, did that come about intentionally, or did some of the symbolism only present itself to you after the quilt was designed or finished?
- You may wish to dialogue with a finished quilt that you feel particularly resonated with who you are. Ask it if any of the images, shapes, colors, blocks, or fabrics have symbolic meaning for you? Ask what messages these elements might have for you? The answer may come right away and flow into your consciousness and onto your journal page, or it may need to percolate. It doesn't hurt to ask, and it could be very revealing!

CONSIDER SETTING A FEW GOALS RELATED TO THE PURPOSE OF YOUR NEXT QUILT.

ASK & JOURNAL:
- Take into account any or all of these factors: where it will be used, the feeling of the quilt, whether you'd like consistency or a break from your previous style, and whether you'd like to try any new techniques?
- Darra approached that part consciously, and then started to just go with the flow, touching fabrics, looking at books, seeing what resonated, sketching roughly, and working on a design wall from one point out, using only fabrics on hand. Try any parts of this approach that feel intuitively good to you. Feel free to just get started like this and then proceed however you feel inspired.
- Darra considers 2012 her most creatively adventurous and fruitful year. Rather than keeping her New Year's resolution private, she announced on her blog her commitment to spend at least 30 minutes *every day* doing something creative. She hit a few bumps along the road–opportunities to blog about how she overcame challenges *"…and then the day came when the risk to remain tight in a bud was more painful than the risk it took to blossom."* She'd always loved that quote from French author and diarist Anais Nin. Never, however, had she felt the connection more strongly. So she took that joy of self-discovery and expressed it in *Bloom* (on the preceding page). Is there a motivation for you in this story? A self-discovery that might come from a quilt you've already made or one you'd like to make to express what you're learning about yourself?

SHARE: I'd love to have you email chris@reapasyousew.com about what you learned from starting with a spiritual descriptor or concept and/or setting some goals relating to your quilt's purpose.

Hong Oridney: Anxiety Relieved through Quiltmaking

Driving my minivan home after seeing my gynecologist, I began to wonder what my physical ailments were telling me. I needed shoulder surgery to repair a torn rotator cuff, and I needed bladder surgery because of damage from prolonged labor. Now my gynecologist said I needed a hysterectomy and eventually a rectal seal. Oblivious that no doctor would agree to such a thing, I was hoping to arrange one walloping surgery and get it all fixed at once. What was I thinking? Maybe that I was indispensable to my globetrotting husband, our 12- and 14-year-old daughters, and my little suburban world? Hence, the desire to minimize my total time out of commission. Maybe I was also dreaming that if I had enough procedures done at once, someone would finally realize I was about to break down and would come to my rescue.

Two years earlier our family had moved to Orinda, a San Francisco suburb, to live closer to my husband's new work base. Toby was already working in San Francisco, so I handled the move by myself. Crying and refusing to leave Newport Beach, our girls barricaded themselves in their rooms as the moving van pulled away with our belongings. The Orinda transition hadn't been easy for any of us. Breaking in socially had been tough for our daughter Kacie, who was at that tender middle school age, and for our younger daughter Brenna, who was switching from a holistic, nurturing Waldorf school to a public school fourth-grade class taught by a drill sergeant who harped on math processing speed. My understanding that Toby's company had committed to paying for the move turned out to be wrong, and two years later we were still financially compromised by the whopping costs.

Although the move was behind us, we were still adjusting. I was doing battle on Brenna's behalf, researching special education law, keeping abreast of her educational testing results, and meeting with school administrators who at first didn't want to provide her with in-class accommodations because her grades were too average to qualify her for federally mandated accommodations. In addition, I'd not only joined the Orinda Newcomers Club; I'd quickly become its president. I'd succumbed to earnest requests to serve on my new church's council. I hosted a rehearsal dinner for forty-two at our house, produced five auction quilts for a school fundraiser, and volunteered in the middle school cafeteria one day a week. Occasionally I wrote legal briefs for my old law practice, and I was the family liaison for a New Jersey lawsuit over my mother-in-law's decline after an accident near her Princeton home. Since we'd moved her to California, I was also visiting her and taking her to doctor's appointments—all that plus parenting, often acting as sole parent because of Toby's work. And I was hardly sleeping, partly because of my racing mind and partly because of searing shoulder pain.

At this point you're probably wondering if I'd lost my mind, piling on more commitments. I now realize that one of a mind's responsibilities is to make choices and set limits that honor the needs of the body and soul. Toby kept pointing out that I was compulsively taking on more and more responsibility, but to me his assessment lacked

Kacie, Chris, and Brenna during the making of *Hong Oridney*. Photo by Toby Smith.

Copyright 1999 by Chris Boersma Smith,
Blah in Your Face (48" x 41").
One of three quilts made in color study classes with Angie Woolman prior to her Design Me class, this piece emerged from a workshop about using neutrals. I found it all so blah that I threw in some coral, and Angie commented that it was certainly in your face for a neutrals quilt!

credibility since he traveled through multiple time zones to Asia and Australia and back so often that the flight attendants recognized him. He never remained home for more than a week or two. Both of us were living insane lives. My body was showing serious strain in a number of ways, and if I'd been able to see myself clearly, I'd have had to admit that my soul was starving.

When I signed up for Angie Woolman's quilt class Design Me: The Elements, however, it wasn't about opting to *slow down and open up*, which is what quilting often does for me, or about consciously seeking creative nurturance as an antidote to the adrenalized life I led. Having learned that no doctor would sign off on simultaneous surgeries, I'd elected to have my rotator cuff repaired first. Knowing I wouldn't be able to play tennis as usual, I simply plugged Angie's class into tennis's vacated space on my calendar. I had no idea where this choice would lead me or that my life would get even more stressful.

Toby and I mostly stayed in touch by e-mail when he was traveling, but one day I telephoned him in Bangkok. I'd been at home resting in bed, recovering from the prior week's shoulder surgery, waiting for someone from my quilt group to drop off dinner. I answered a phone call from the dermatologist I'd seen ten days earlier for a routine skin check. The pathology report had come back from a biopsy I'd insisted on for a tan growth the doctor characterized as "nothing." The news was anything but; I had melanoma. The good news was that the cancer had been detected early. Toby sounded full of regret as he attempted to reassure me, but it was 12-year-old Brenna who became my comforter while I dealt with the initial shock. I scheduled the excision for a week later on the day after Toby was due home. It didn't even occur to me to ask him to risk the displeasure of his superiors to come home early nor, to him, to disrupt the dealings he was involved in to jump on a plane. Our obligations, many of them self-imposed, trumped even our marriage and our health.

How did I get to this place where my response to clear warning signs that my life was in serious danger was simply to go faster and harder, to deny that I needed a sane life? The oldest of five children born in a ten-year span, I had a father who was on the road selling advertising Monday through Friday and a consequently overburdened mother, so I learned early not to expect to get my emotional needs met. If I wanted parental attention, I felt my choices were either to act out—a role already claimed by some of my siblings, which netted them attention but not the kind I had in mind—or to seek approval. I chose to conform to Dad's number-one rule, "If you can't put on a happy face, then go to your room." I put on the people-pleasing demeanor. I started down the long self-improvement road. And I tried to earn love by accomplishing as much as I could. My controlling mindset (which in retrospect I know was based on false beliefs) was that I wasn't good enough, nor was I loved just for who I was. Of course, we don't automatically leave those childhood thoughts and adaptations behind when we reach adulthood, because we're seldom conscious of them.

So here I was still trying to please, deferring what I desperately needed—rest, nurturance, balance, a real marriage—to a vague time in the future when I would earn or deserve all that, when life would somehow slow down, when someone would realize I was drowning and pull me out. The truth was that I'd long ago lost any sense of what I needed or even the inner permission to ask myself what my needs might be. I'm not unique in this. Maybe by now you recognize yourself in this story. Or maybe you recognize your partner. Men and women can have their own versions of this affliction.

When Toby was hired to coordinate the San Francisco private equity firm's Australian business, he was to be considered for partnership after a nine-month trial. We took what we thought was a low-risk gamble in selling our Newport Beach house and buying in the Bay Area without waiting for partnership, thus eliminating Toby's California commute and, we hoped, giving him that time at home. The most senior partner had reiterated over several lavish interview dinners, "What matters most in the end is family. Love is what life's all about," so we assumed that a level of commitment to family values existed at the firm's highest level.

After a year of quarterly trips to Sydney, Toby began putting together a consortium of institutional investors from around the world for a new project in Thailand, and his work life went into warp speed. He conducted extensive negotiations with businesspeople, civil servants, and a team of translators and lawyers. Nothing happened quickly, and a large part of the success of his firm depended on his efforts. Offices in Hong Kong, Bangkok, and Sydney had to be staffed and managed, and some of the management team got along like oil and water. With a twenty-two-hour trip from home to hotel, a seventeen-hour time difference, and conference calls at all hours from whichever continent he was on, Toby was working day and night. As if his daily work wasn't enough, he was ordered to pass arduous financial analyst exams. No wonder he, too, was developing physical symptoms of stress, including a mysterious and painful lump about which he'd had no time to see a doctor.

Even on the ten to fourteen days a month when Toby was home, I didn't consider him truly present. He'd sit in one armchair the entire day, catching up on e-mails, studying, and reading all the newspapers accumulated in his absence. Lonely, I craved a social life as well as companionship with my husband. More than anything, I wanted to feel like a real married couple. I had a new acquaintance whose husband traveled most weeks, and we were eager to get together with our husbands, hoping to forge a connection between couples. After many failed attempts, Toby and I finally found a night when we were free to accept their invitation. Excited, I dolled myself up to go out. At their home that Saturday evening, Toby nodded off at the dinner table.

I'd about had it. "I'd never have had children if I thought I was going to be a single mother so much of the time," I lamented. "The girls need you around more. I hate being the disciplinarian all by myself. And we all miss you. We had no idea when you accepted this job that you'd end up with an office, a secretary, and permanent worker status in Thailand. We're in debt from the move. We have no social life, no romance, and you're killing yourself."

We each felt at the mercy of other people and angry at the situation, but there was no easy fix. Toby told me he'd been thinking hard about how to accommodate the enormous needs of this new business venture, negotiate office dynamics, and prove himself on one hand and to conscientiously care for and be with his family on the other. Why didn't he just find another job? The current one seemed the best means of providing for us, and finding another good job in his field without travel and at his age seemed impossible. Besides, his own childhood had rendered primary his commitment to his role as provider, and his current work seemed likely to yield a long-term payoff. As a new partner, he was reluctant to ask for special favors despite his deep desire to accommodate family needs, and that left him in serious conflict. For my part, my deepest desire was to avoid the dad-out-of-town-and-mom-losing-it family model I'd grown up with. Something had to give.

So in another grasp at family togetherness, we began to explore whether we should move to the other side of the world where Toby was spending so much of his time. But where? And how would we convince the senior partners to support us? Notwithstanding their "family first" talk, they took Toby's travel for granted. They poured company resources into fine food and wines and fancy ski trips, but they'd not offered to pay for our previous move to keep our family together. And how did we know if living in a foreign city would be good for all of us?

Before the first meeting of Angie Woolman's class, I accompanied Toby to Asia to scope out what it might be like to live there. While he worked in Bangkok, I flew to Hong Kong. I researched neighborhoods and schools, house-hunted, and talked with expatriate families about logistics and lifestyle, I thought about the impact of my own experience as an exchange student and what it might mean for our daughters to have the opportunity to live in another culture. I ultimately picked up school applications and noted the approaching deadlines. Soon after we returned home, we sent in Hong Kong International School applications just in case.

Designs Began with Inspirational Photos and Favorite Fabrics

When Design Me: The Elements began in mid-February 2000, we'd been living for two months in anxious uncertainty about where we'd end up. Unfocused as to how, when, where, and whether this move would happen, I wondered obsessively what our future would look like. Back in the present, Angie had a plan for us—to start with a single inspirational photograph, to cut into fabric without using a ruler, and to begin with primitive shapes. The supply list had suggested bringing pictures of nature, architecture, people, shapes, or whatever else might appeal to us–and a variety of fabrics. During the course of five classes, we'd be working in a series, making one top every six weeks, finishing at the end of May with three art quilts. We'd start designing and making the first quilt in the first class, but we'd be doing most of the work at home between the sessions.

Before we even settled on which of our pictures might be the springboard for our first quilt in the series, Angie had us pull out ten favorite fabrics of similar value, dive in, and free-cut strips, piecing them together randomly to make a strata. I inhaled, braced myself, and sliced into an expensive contemporary print fabric. Thinking its undulating bands so elegant, I'd hoarded it for a couple of years in my stash, preserving it for fear that something so beautiful wouldn't ever come to me again. I added purples and teals I'd long collected. I found myself surprised that I'd actually put such precious fabric in with my class supplies. Fleetingly I wondered if an unconscious muse or Spirit had slipped that fabric in and given me the courage to cut it without a defined end in mind, risking wasting it.

Next I flipped through the pictures I'd brought and pulled out a Sydney Opera House postcard. I'd nursed a drink one day at a café along Circular Quay and was mesmerized by the opera house perched on its promontory, its elliptical white shells of various sizes flanked by the azure sea, the Sydney Harbour Bridge as its backdrop. Its majesty moved me, but *why* eluded me at the time. Since Angie had instructed us to start by selecting from our photographs certain shapes we liked and then progress in the series to shapes representing experience, I intuitively chose the opera house. Then I selected fabrics in different values of blue to make a strata for the opera house's shells. (They were actually white but the light can give them a blue cast.)

The Opera House, Sydney, Australia. Photo by Toby Smith

Chris Boersma Smith

Hong Kong Cultural Centre with clock tower.
© Depositphotos.com/leungchopan.

Angie's idea was to use just one shape from one photograph, but an inner pull led me to also extract from my class supplies a postcard of the Hong Kong Cultural Centre. Once the two photos were in front of me, I knew I wanted to make this art quilt about my confused state of mind, a snarl of images of different cities, any of which might be our home at this time next year. I just needed a picture to represent Orinda, so I e-mailed Toby (a better photographer than I am), asking him to photograph the downtown theater marquee the next time he was home. Before we left class that first day, I'd sewn my dark background strata and settled on my theme. Angie told us to keep this first quilt abstract, to focus on the chosen shape, and to return to the next class with a finished top.

Orinda Theatre at night, Orinda, CA

Making Images Helped Emotions to Be Recognized and Spirit to Assist

Back home I designed the quilt's appliqués on paper. My inner urgings were stronger than my usual people-pleasing habit, and I followed them without hesitating. My approach was not analytical in the least for a change. I didn't weigh alternatives to come up with my composition. Rather, my state of mind was jumbled, and likewise the images just seemed to want to squash themselves into a single pile on my strata background. I went with it because it spoke to me. I began to understand how much I wished the cities were all merged into one because then Toby would be there, and so would the girls and I. The name for the piece, Hong Oridney, came to me as I looked at the juxtaposed buildings from HONG Kong, ORInda, and SyDNEY. That's what I wanted—no more separation, no more raging anxiety. Our family, not separate but one. United. Together. In one spot.

The composition was intuitive, but the complete design did not evolve quickly. The first class had been on February 21. I made some sketches and created the pale strata, but the final drawing wasn't done until the tail end of March. Toby's lump was still undiagnosed, and I was calling it a tumor in my journal. In the daytime I'd remind myself to trust and wait, but at night sleep remained elusive.

When I started using tracing paper to commingle the shapes of the buildings, I found myself drawing in detail. Maybe because our situation was so abstract and unresolved, I wanted realism in parts of my design, although this was not a conscious choice. The placement of the central images wasn't realistic because the three buildings grew like branches out of a single trunk, with the wall of the cultural centre wrapping them all like a ribbon around a tree. Yet the buildings I sketched bore very similar texture to the actual wall's blocks, the tower's bricks, the marquee's art deco friezes, and the chevron-patterned tiles of the opera house shells. With the drawing enlarged, I began selecting fabrics from which I'd execute the images in appliqué. I was drawn to the places' actual colors and excited to recreate the clock and cornerstones of the tower. I found an organza to create some shade to set off the doors of the opera house. I envisioned quilting those chevrons onto the opera house and embroidering the face on the clock. I was enjoying the way the images were taking shape into a piece that had real meaning for me. I'd completely forgotten the assignment to use strata throughout to build an abstract shape.

While I was feeling helpless to influence the most important issue in my life, I worked deliberately, manipulating the fabric for each building, exercising control over these creative decisions. As I handled the pieces representing the various cities, I considered the pros and cons of living in each. Although Thailand was where most of the work was, I didn't think we could live in steamy Bangkok with its difficult language, serious pollution, and very foreign culture. So I didn't represent it in my quilt. Sydney is a beautiful, fun, English-speaking city with beaches and great weather—all definite pluses. Sydney to Bangkok flights are only a third as long as the Bangkok trip from California, and conference calls wouldn't be at dinnertime; however, Sydney would still mean having Toby away many weekdays. On the pro side for Hong Kong, much of the firm's Asian work was there, and Bangkok could be a day trip or just an overnight stay. The city would be culturally enriching and probably advantageous for the girls' not-so-far-off college applications. We could get along well with English. We could live with a view of the gorgeous South China Sea. It was safe, and the expatriate community was welcoming. As for the cons, it could be muggy. It was crowded, and it was expensive. I knew the pluses and minuses of Orinda.

I machine-stitched the movie names from the theater photograph onto my fabric marquee. Continuing the fantasy that Hong Kong, Sydney, and Orinda were in a single spot in time and place, my photograph had captured a moment in time when *Erin Brockovich*, *Cider House Rules*, and *The Price of Glory* were in the movie theaters. That last title triggered a spark of resentment as I wondered if all this turmoil was the price of glory in Toby's career. Yet Toby isn't about ego and greed. He's a driven provider because of his own experience as a young man, but he's also eager to make a societal difference. Through expansion of local businesses, new employment opportunities, and responsible corporate governance and environmental policies, the fund he was building was becoming a major contributor to bettering the lives of tens of thousands of people in the developing world. Although it helped to know the motivation wasn't glory, it remained true that Toby's drivenness clashed with my longing to be together.

Inspiration, Insight, and Open Doors Came As the First Quilt Neared Completion

At the final assembly phase of the quilt top, I'd lie in bed, get an idea, and thank God for inspiration. I knew I was growing through the process of making this quilt—not just as a quiltmaker but inwardly as well. It finally dawned on me that the quilt was depicting living in the unknown. The quiltmaking process was allowing me to move general anxiety outside my body into something tangible in a way that helped me achieve personal clarity. What we needed to resolve was not the whole future (as if that were even a possibility) but rather just one multiple-choice question, "In which city would we be living when the next school year started?"

I wanted to include in my quilt a key to my mental state, so I asked Toby to get a colleague to write in Chinese the original question we'd been asking. The day after this man handed me a piece of paper on which he'd written the characters depicting the phrase "What does the future hold?" he suffered multiple brain aneurysms. He's been unable to speak or work ever since. I embroidered his characters onto the quilt, a reminder that we never know what tomorrow may bring. I vowed to make a supreme effort to live each day fully in the present. (But vows set a mighty goal, and in hindsight, I was only able to handle tiny steps.)

All during my work at home I prayed to live faithfully in the present while petitioning, "Lord, open the doors you want opened, close the doors you want closed." And I stayed alert to see whatever signs might appear. Circumstances were changing

Chris Boersma Smith

Copyright 2002 by Chris Boersma Smith, *Hong Oridney I* (52" x 49")

but not dictating a particular outcome yet. Toby had visited a doctor, and the lump was growing. Although no biopsy had been done, I was sweating the idea that he had a long-neglected tumor. Surely that would keep him in the United States and off planes. Yet his firm had just decided to sell its North American interests and to focus solely on Asia, rendering his work there more crucial than ever. It also meant organizational restructuring was likely.

The most powerful senior partner was starting to shift some responsibilities around, and many were landing on Toby. When Kacie was accepted into the Hong Kong school but Brenna was put on a mile-long waiting list, I considered homeschooling Brenna. Perhaps that was the solution for her learning differences. I also considered that it might indicate that the move to Hong Kong was not meant to be.

Doing It Wrong Was Right, and Doing It Right Was Meaningless

At the start of the second class in the Design Me series, I pinned up my finished quilt top, and frankly I expected praise. What I heard instead was Angie telling me that I hadn't followed the instructions because my shapes were not abstract and my design was too complex. *Certainly my deeper self had sensed what I needed and had overridden her instructions. But now, was this an inspired voice telling me the answer was simpler than it seemed?* I went home and began to work the image a second time in a more abstract way, producing *Hong Oridney II*.

Discussions among Toby's partners became heated. By the completion of this second quilt, Sydney was no longer a possibility because of both a personnel change and the increasing priority of Asia. I decided that hot colors would represent Hong Kong, cool colors everything else. Angie instructed us to use all solids, and my newly feisty spirit deviated a bit and chose polka dots that appeared solid from a distance. I finished that top and quilted it quickly—even before I'd finished quilting Hong Oridney I. I didn't feel anything special for it though, and it's never been hung.

Circumstances Came Together, and Uncertainty Was Resolved

Between the second and third classes I'd noticed that this quiltmaking had reduced my anxiety by focusing me on just a couple of alternatives; however, I still didn't have a fulfilling marriage and family life, and I hadn't given up trying to attain them. So at a company dinner at a Carmel restaurant during a firm outing, I decided to lobby the senior partner. From what Toby had told me, he refused to acknowledge the stress our family was under because of so much separation, and he didn't want to approve a realistic budget for a move. Yet since he was the ostensible champion of family values and he was under the influence of some of the world's finest wines, I thought I could get away with being blunt better than Toby could. The senior partner was not receptive. He savagely dressed me down, asserting contemptuously that Toby wasn't working or traveling too much and that I was overreacting when I claimed that stress was killing our family. He was like a malevolent warlord, and he issued an unveiled physical threat against "anyone who would oppose him." Shocked to my core, I fled to the ladies' room and sobbed until I needed tinted glasses and a colleague's wife to coax me back to the table. Because this man had the most clout in the firm, it was now clear that if Toby pushed him for a transfer to Asia, it would be career suicide. A door had slammed shut.

As ugly a scene as it was, the confrontation clarified everything. Toby saw the extent of my pain and his boss's hypocrisy. He resolved not to sacrifice his family to a superior's self-serving rule and complete lack of compassion. He strategized with me about how he could gain more say in managing his travel without risking his job. Investors were designating him as a key man in their long-term contracts, so he was gaining leverage. He dropped the financial analyst studies, which were time-consuming and irrelevant to his work. At the same time we noticed how our own compulsions were affecting our attitudes and behaviors, and we also noticed the games being played all around us. With awareness came some relief.

Between the second and third classes of Design Me, as Toby and I ceased lobbying to go overseas as a family, management realigned within the firm both in San Francisco and in Asia. Strong Bangkok leadership and staff members were assembled to take on much of the day-to-day work there. Toby had to devote more time to California investor relations. Fortunately his suspected tumor turned out to be a cyst, and he was feeling well again. Thanks to answered prayers, I no longer needed a hysterectomy or bladder surgery. I thank God that this miraculous healing has continued for more than a decade! Because I'd channeled my anxiety into both creativity and prayer while I was waiting, I began to trust that the outcome was just as it should have been, and I was greatly relieved to have the uncertainty resolved.

For the final quilt in the series, which I started but then didn't complete until twenty months after the last design class, I created another concept quilt by using piecing and appliqué based on a composite of photographed images—realistic parts comprising an imaginary whole. This third quilt was also about how Toby's work affected us. By the time he got his Asia fund successfully launched, I'd completed *Khorp khun Ka, Meung Thai* (*Thank you, Thailand*) in gratitude for the fund's closing—the culmination of two years of negotiations and patience. I'd begun to relate Toby's dedication to his role as provider to the image of the mythical figure who held up the temple wall—a mosaic against stone that I'd seen at the Grand Palace in Bangkok. It seemed to me that Toby was holding up his company (represented by its logo) and dozens of its employees' families as well as our family. The fund benefits public pensioners in California and in three Asian countries. On an even broader level, his work has improved US-Thai relations and supported thousands of Thai workers and their families, represented in this third quilt by a Bangkok-inspired skyline.

Copyright 2002 Chris Boersma Smith, *Khorp khun Ka, Meung Thai* (*Thank you, Thailand*) (37" x 52")

Neither the Quilts Nor Life Were Black and White

Just as the three quilts were neither realistic nor black and white, how Toby and I handled that Hong Oridney time, the choices we made and the ones we failed to make, cannot be judged in retrospect as right or wrong, good or bad. The stresses inherent in Toby's work and my acceleration and overload in response to stress rendered our perspective myopic. We felt at the mercy of the circumstances, and like most people in crisis, we alternately reacted and simply coped. Today, looking at these quilts, reflecting back, and telling this story, I see that the more balls I try to juggle, the more my attention has to stay on the balls, the less opportunity there is to slow down and feel the emotions obscured by the chaos. We all resist pain, but it turns out that the struggle to ward off painful feelings adds suffering, takes up precious mental space, and prevents resolution. I tried to deal with the chaos in my heart and mind with capability, order, responsibility, and busyness. I tried to control it.

What actually worked was to acknowledge what was going on inside by creating emotionally-inspired images that showed me my fear, confusion, and longing and made space for Spirit to come to my aid. Discovering in this creative way just how frightened and unanchored I felt and allowing myself to know my aching sadness (about my children not having their father and my not having my husband with us more) freed me from my anxiety and opened the way for a measure of clarity, dialogue, and serenity.

Spirit's Promptings Rescued and Affirmed Me

In addition, while I was receiving Angie Woolman's guidelines for the class as a whole, an unseen teacher was apparently instructing me personally. In this case, it was through taking time for myself, breaking the rules, and honoring inner promptings that I finally came to awareness, and as a bonus, I created two quilts that both helped and pleased me. Now I'm able to employ the process consciously, particularly at times of deep-seated emotional conflict. Quiltmaking with Spirit, as I did here, allows me to actively participate in my own rescue without having to do the impossible, hoping someone else will realize I need help.

Another wonderful aspect of sharing this story has been my wonder about why the opera house called to me. Spiritual mentors have told me that when someone or something holds an inordinate attraction or repulsion for us, we should consider how that person or thing mirrors our self, and learn from it. So I recently sat on my window seat in Sea Ranch and dialogued with the Sydney Opera House and it revealed how much we share. For example, when I'm in our Sea Ranch home, the opera house and I are both perched oceanside, often alone. Although our façades exhibit a strength and grace, what's going on inside is a mystery to many. We are multi-purpose gems of inspired design, at least from our creators' viewpoints! The opera house then spoke to me in the following poem:

> I have strong structure and soft curves.
> Be glad that you do too, woman.
> I open my doors and invite others in. You can too.
> I fill my halls with music and dance.
> Fill yours with such joy also!
> I sit still and let the light shine on me.
> Do the same, with a capital L.
> I represent creative art, innovation, and
> transcendent beauty. You create that, too.
> I am uplifting and inspiring. So are you.
> The Sydney Harbour Bridge and
> I are landmarks together,
> and this partner doesn't dwarf me.
> Likewise, you are not less significant in this
> world than your husband and his work.
> I must be preserved, and so must you.

Copyright 2008 by Chris Boersma Smith, *Down Under* (17" x 17"). The lighter shape is an icon of the Sydney Opera House facing four directions, while the dark arches echo the curves of the Sydney Harbour Bridge.

--- STEPS ALONG A SPIRITUAL QUILTMAKING PATH ---

CONSIDER THAT AN IMAGE THAT MESMERIZES OR REPELS YOU IS OFTEN A MIRROR FOR ASPECTS OF YOURSELF. Consider letting such an image inspire a quilt for the purpose of self-discovery. The quilt could be abstract or realistic. It doesn't matter.

FIRST SMALL ACTION: Just begin with the image, perhaps in a design journal. Sit with it, your eyes closed, and let your imagination go. If other images or associations come to you, put them in your design journal too. You might even wish to pose a question to the thing, and sit in silence to see if you receive certain words or an insight.

CREATE: Select fabrics that evoke the emotions you feel, and start creating. If you've made small drawings, they can be taken to a copy center and blown up onto architectural sized paper to make appliqué templates. You could abstract the design or keep it more realistic. For a quicker project, you could fuse Wonder-Under backed fabric that's been cut and pressed onto a whole-cloth or pieced background. Of course, you could use your usual style and technique, or you could let go and play with an attitude that this will be an interesting exercise regardless of the finished product.

* * *

CONSIDER HOW QUILTMAKING CAN FACILITATE SPIRITUAL DISCERNMENT.

ASK & JOURNAL: Invite your higher power to work with you in the discernment process, to guide you, and to open and close the doors that will lead to the highest and best outcome for all concerned. You may wish to pray, meditate, journal, or simply sit in silence for about twenty minutes before you start each day's creative work.

CREATE: If you're facing a decision and wish to discern an answer, try making a quilt about the state of not knowing or about alternatives. In doing so, pay attention to how you may hone in on what's of central importance. Follow your intuition or Spirit's guidance. Pay attention to images, dreams, or even colors that come to you and want to be expressed. Be open to mental pro and con lists that may come as you work and to doors that open and close in your outer world. Check in with your body to see if it has messages for you.

* * *

CONSIDER QUILTMAKING AS A CONSCIOUS ANTIDOTE: For example, working on a quilt you can control while others parts of your life seem more out of control than usual can provide calm in the storm.

CREATE:
- If you feel out of control, create a wish-quilt, where you depict elements as you might wish them to be, working deliberately, giving fantasy and imagination free reign.
- If you're in a state of unrest, work on something soothing.
- If you're in a state of boredom or your life seems a little dull, bring in some excitement by challenging yourself to create a wild, exotic, or bright piece with a lot of movement, stretching yourself to experiment with new techniques or design challenges.

Hope for Our World: Hollis's Social Activism

In her suburban Philadelphia backyard, the girl who would become the leading fiber artist promoting worldwide social and environmental issues looked skyward at every passing plane and wondered about its destination. Hollis Chatelain was born and raised in Berwyn, PA, where she and I both attended Conestoga Senior High; however, she entered after I graduated, and we weren't acquainted then. I took all the home economics I could at that school. Teenaged Hollis couldn't sew and didn't care to learn. My mother stressed the importance of tidy seams and obligatory churchgoing. Hollis's mother, aunts, and grandmother perceived with extraordinary intuition. Hollis became accustomed to spirituality as rudimentary, though she never entered a place of worship until she was 26 and has only attended a handful of special occasion church services.

Hollis often remembered her vibrant dreams. She didn't envision, however, that she would create internationally acclaimed quilts that would grace public and private collections in Europe, Asia, South America, Africa, and North America … or that her dreams would be her greatest source of inspiration. And she had no inkling that outside her family her most formative and fulfilling relationship would be with Africa.

In addition to its roots in her dreams and her wanderlust, Hollis's art career evolved by accident … or providence. Partway through college she transferred to Drexel University. In order to maximize transfer credits, she switched her major to design, even though she'd never done art before. Working four years part-time as a photographer and darkroom specialist, Hollis realized how much she preferred photography over a job as an interior or fashion designer. Her passion for taking pictures, her desire to board a plane to a far-off land, and her desire for change after a breakup propelled Hollis to join the Peace Corps in 1980. Camera in tow, she set off to Togo to capture images of its people on film … and to serve as an agricultural education volunteer. Hollis learned more than she taught. Her personal life and social activism were about to develop into something with far more impact than the thousands of striking photos she shot.

Four years before Hollis joined the Peace Corps, a young man named Reynald rode his bicycle from his native Switzerland to sub-Saharan Africa. He came upon a small Togolese village and decided to stay for a week, but he was still there when Hollis arrived. As the only two white people in the village, they were destined to meet. For Hollis it was love at first sight, and the whole village encouraged their relationship. They married, worked, and lived in four West African, French-speaking countries—Togo for two years, Burkina Faso for five, Mali for three, and Benin for two—and they also lived two years in Switzerland. They raised three children, all born in Africa, the first two biologically theirs, the youngest adopted.

Hollis and Reynald's fourteen years together overseas were devoted to hands-on assistance to African people, and that devotion continues now in the United States. Here, though, it's a different kind of hands-on work. Hollis's labor of creating textile art to help others see the joy, beauty, and harmony of Africa is an attempt to counterbalance the negative images that prevail in the Western world. In 1996, when they moved stateside, Reynald gave up his career to free Hollis to create while he handles the office aspects of Hollis's career as well as many family responsibilities.

Let's go back to Africa and see how the Peace Corps volunteer with a passion for photography became a textile artist. Although most think of Africa as a place of need, for Hollis it was a place of discovery. In the beginning, traveling to remote locations and walking around the villages, Hollis would speak French with the people, getting to know them so that they were comfortable with her before she photographed them. She took pictures of children playing, women mothering, younger men working, older men sitting, as well as trees, mosques, baskets, and markets.

Copyright 1998 by Hollis Chatelain, *Rolling Toys* (54" x 48"). Whole cloth, hand-dye-painted and machine-quilted, based on Hollis's photos and memories of happy children playing with tires, perhaps the most common toy in West Africa.

In their second post, Burkina Faso, the government wanted to limit Westerners from taking pictures that might reinforce poor impressions of their country, so they required a photography permit, which took a week of long lines to obtain and expired in thirty days. Consequently Hollis found a new outlet for her creativity in this overlooked, landlocked country of 17 million people and a capital whose name rolls off the tongue like a name in a nursery rhyme, Ouagadougou.

"Fabric was like gold in West Africa," she says. "I had my clothes made by the Burkinabè tailors, and I loved to hang around and talk with them. They were throwing away scraps of this beautiful fabric, and finally I asked for some. I wanted to learn to do something with it, so I bought a book and a sewing machine and started teaching myself and the local women to do patchwork." Although it was the love of African textiles that attracted Hollis to textile art, she wasn't destined to become a traditional quilter.

Hollis also began drawing, even doing some portraits. Hollis told me that she really *sees* the person she's drawing and that an energy of intimacy grows between artist and subject. She drew many of her friends and also became friends with many of her subjects. They taught Hollis the difference one individual can make in bringing healing to a hurting person, family, village, nation, or world. When Reynald was severely ill, their African friends would come sit with them, hold their hands, and offer moral support, even at some risk of contagion. That experience profoundly affects Hollis's view of social activism. Where some might see overwhelming poverty and feel hopeless, Hollis and Reynald see that each person can do a small part to improve the situation. Every drop of water is part of what fills the bucket.

Hollis drawing in Africa

Although their work in Africa was fulfilling, by 1996 Hollis and Reynald felt it was time to take their children to the United States for their higher education. They chose Hillsborough, NC, where they bought an old farmhouse with room to add a studio. Six months after the move Hollis missed Africa so much that she started to paint African images on fabric, embarking on her figurative and nature series of dye-painted and heavily quilted art. She was following her heart and going on faith that this could also produce a living for her family.

Reap As You Sew

Hollis's Life as a Textile Artist in America

Hollis gets up before the sun and exercises. Except when she's on the road teaching and lecturing on quilting, color, drawing, West African textiles, and inspiration and activism in art, she works in her studio seven days a week. She puts in twelve- to fourteen-hour days, breaking only to pay attention to her children (when they were still at home) and her pets, and she might break for lunch and a late-afternoon swim with her husband in their backyard pool during warm weather. She's done this week after week and month after month because this is her work. She's serious about it, and that's what it takes to meet the exacting standards she sets for herself.

In February 2002, Hollis was in Los Angeles one week after she accepted a handsome offer to sell *Blue Men*, which was then her favorite of all the quilts she'd made. Because she quilts for a living, she'd always intended to sell the piece. She just wasn't ready to let go of it. Reynald was at home, and she needed him to look into her eyes, listen to her feelings, hold her, and help her detach from this six-and-a-half-feet-wide, monochromatic wall-hanging that had taken first place at a Minnesota *Quilting the Quilt* exhibit and turned eyes at Houston's *International Quilt Festival*, where it had won the Masters Award for Contemporary Artistry. *Blue Men* is a *material object*, she reminded herself. But accepting that the quilt would be staying in California felt akin

Copyright 2001 by Hollis Chatelain, *Blue Men* (58" x 78") depicts the nomadic Tuaregs who roam the Sahara Desert on their camels. They wear indigo blue turbans, giving their skin a blue tint. Hollis made this whole cloth quilt as a tribute to a people she admires and respects, including many Tuaregs she counts as friends. This quilt was part of the ten-year retrospective exhibit, *Hollis Chatelain: Unraveling the Myths about Africa through Quilts*.

to dropping a child off at college to start an independent life.

Hollis had noticed that her dreams yield colorful images when she's feeling peaceful but monochromatic people and events when she's disturbed. In L.A. while she was struggling to let go of *Blue Men*, she awoke with a powerful dream, a vivid scene starring Archbishop Desmond Tutu of South Africa. He was walking into a field. Children were coming to him, gazing at him in awe, drawn to him as if he were the Pied Piper. He was there to make everything better, emanating hope for world peace and raising awareness of what the current generation would be leaving for the next. The entire image appeared in purples ranging from light to dark.

All Hollis knew of Desmond Tutu was that he was a prominent religious figure from South Africa, a country she'd never visited. He didn't represent any church to her. Rather, he symbolized hope, a better world, and a future for Hollis, her children, and indeed all children. She couldn't start working on a Desmond Tutu quilt right away though. *Precious Water*, another monochromatic, dream-inspired quilt, needed to be finished first. And she had classes to teach.

I was fortunate to be in two days of Hollis's classes on that California trip. The buyer of *Blue Men* owned a Berkeley quilt shop where Hollis would be teaching. I was in a small weekly quilt group with her, and she told us this was an opportunity not to miss. I showed up, knowing nothing of Hollis. When I saw her quilts, I would have been completely intimidated by this creative genius if I hadn't quickly found out that we'd graduated from the same high school.

During her color and Quilt Line as Third Aspect of Design classes, Hollis said she could teach anyone to draw. Some of us wanted to take her up on the challenge. It would mean committing to years of study with her, and the quilt shop didn't want to sponsor drawing classes. I ended up as the organizer, contracted with Hollis to teach our group, and I have been coordinating and hosting what have evolved into annual masters series workshops that have met from 2003 through the present and expanded into ten-year programs held in various parts of the country (although we've got #13 pending). I soon got to know the person behind the public persona because Hollis would stay with me.

After Drawing I and II, we had a week of Portraiture. Then we combined with a Santa Barbara group for a five-day Color Workshop, where on the first morning Hollis slipped on a stairway and injured her coccyx. Determined not to disappoint mentorees who'd taken off work, traveled, and paid for the class, Hollis taught the class in serious pain. She alternated between sitting on an inner tube and lying on a mattress on the floor with ice stuffed down her unzipped pants. In return, the class worked their tails off, some pulling all-nighters so that they would not let Hollis down and so that they could learn all they possibly could from her. Her just completed *Precious Water* hung in the room to inspire us.

Copyright 2004 by Hollis Chatelain, *Precious Water* (77" x 85") is based on a monochromatic dream about continual droughts threatening our planet. Because fresh water is precious and limited, Hollis's images, painted with dyes using six values of yellow, represent four continents.

Detail of *Hope for Our World* prior to quilting

Detail of *Hope for Our World* after intricate machine quilting

Hollis and I each had bodywork sessions that year with an intuitive woman called Eagle Feather. Comparing our experiences, we discussed our spiritual beliefs. It was not the first time, but here we pinpointed shared beliefs. Although I practice my faith in line with an organized religion and Hollis doesn't, we both see spiritual reality trumping the empirical world. We both sense through our spirits. We accept that our paths in life unfold according to a plan bigger than us. And we frequently see one spiritual believer helping to heal another. We also both accept that the dream world and the spirit of life are inextricably part of the whole. For example, Hollis once asked me to help her interpret a dream about her father getting injured while working on his antique cars in his barn. Another time she sought input on a dream where she was swimming in a beautiful golden swamp with knee-deep water the consistency of melted chocolate and where an elephant gently pushed her away to protect her from a huge crocodile. During the dream she felt peaceful and loved. In each case, thanks to some training I'd garnered in spiritual direction school, I was able to help. The first dream felt like a premonition, so I urged Hollis to warn her father to check out the barn's condition, which helped her father avert injury. Guided by her elephant dream, I interpreted some symbols that helped her make a good business decision.

The Making of Hope for Our World

With a composition in mind straight from a dream, Hollis first draws what she saw. She may also work from various photographs for parts of the scene. She fastidiously refines a line drawing on paper before she projects it onto fabric she's prepared for dye-painting. Next she uses thickened fabric dyes in various values of one color. With many paintbrushes and meticulous attention to detail, she paints the whole cloth and lets it dry. After washing the dye-painted cloth and sandwiching the top with batting and a back, she begins to audition and select hundreds of threads. With up to fourteen miles of thread per quilt, she machine stitches her images to life.

So after the Desmond Tutu dream Hollis researched her subject matter, looked at photographs of the archbishop, and talked to a biographer to make sure he'd wear purple. When she finally got the Desmond Tutu piece to the drawing stage, Hollis felt it wasn't coming together to her satisfaction. Something was missing. She sensed that she needed contact with the archbishop himself. She thought she'd write to him to see about some opportunity to meet. Her heart and mind were set on it. But first she had to go to Paducah. The Museum of the American Quilter's Society was hosting a solo exhibit of her work called *Living Messages.*

Quilt show vendors' area in Paducah, KY. Photo courtesy of Country Heritage Tours, www.countryheritagetours.com

Hollis was working in a booth doing a thread demonstration at the AQS show when a woman approached and invited her to come lecture at Berea College. Noisy sewing machines and exclamations of shopping quilters blocked out every other word. Hollis thought she heard the woman say that the Dalai Lama had come and that Desmond Tutu would be coming and—

"Excuse me? What did you say? Can we make an appointment to talk?" Hollis asked, harnessing her attention.

They met the next day. The woman, Alina Strand, was the director of international education. Her job involved grants, visas, scholarships, and the nurturing of foreign students (ninety-four that year out of a student body of 1,500) at a Christian college in Berea, Kentucky. And Hollis's ears had not deceived her. Archbishop Desmond Tutu was due at Berea in three weeks to speak at the school's commencement. But there were huge obstacles to meeting him.

Alina asked Hollis to e-mail her a written request to meet with the archbishop and to include her reasons for requesting the meeting. She said that she'd present the request and said, "Maybe we can see about this." She was not promising. And even if a meeting could be set up, Hollis had committed to be a juror for *Fine Art Quilts 2005,* being held in Memphis the same weekend.

Hollis and Reynald checked flights and MapQuest. Berea was a seven-hour drive from Memphis, eight hours from Hollis's home, and not even close to any airport most Americans had ever heard of. To fly there from Memphis would cost $1,000 in airfare and rebooking penalties.

Hollis and Reynald waited for two weeks. No word.

One week before the graduation Hollis heard that Archbishop Tutu was interested in meeting her, but the only possible time he had was his Saturday evening prayer time. She was told the older man had a protective entourage who didn't like him to be overscheduled. If he were tired by then, the meeting wouldn't take place. She told herself a private audience might not be necessary. Perhaps it would be enough to hear his commencement address. Unfortunately no assurances came even for that possibility. If it rained, only students and their parents would see him in person. Everyone else would have to watch on closed circuit TV.

"Is it worth a thousand dollars to maybe meet him, maybe get an audience, and maybe end up merely seeing him on television?" Reynald asked. Hollis nodded. She contacted the Memphis quilt show and managed to get the judging schedule adjusted so that she could complete her duties there on Saturday morning, allowing her to fly to Berea for the tentative evening meeting. Now she needed a room in a college town that had only one inn that was always booked solid a year in advance for graduation. The next day there was a cancellation! Alina secured the room for her, and the college was paying the tab.

On the way to her hotel in Memphis, Reynald called to tell Hollis he'd heard that her meeting with the archbishop was confirmed for seven o'clock Sunday morning; however, the message was garbled, and where to meet was not specified. When Hollis arrived Saturday evening, she left the archbishop a message at the front desk. Before she turned in at eleven, the envelope was still in his mailbox. She lay awake until three o'clock and barely slept after that. She decided not to plan what to say. She simply wanted to be in his presence. If she could feel his energy, she knew she'd be able to create him in her quilt. Perhaps the best way for her to communicate with him was to show him not only her portfolio and postcards of a number of her quilts but also one he could touch. She chose *Jimmy Carter: Ambassador of Peace*.

Copyright 2005 by Hollis Chatelain, *Jimmy Carter—Ambassador of Peace* (26" x 42")

At 6:50 a.m., Hollis was dressed and ready in the lobby, but her message was still undelivered. At seven thirty, she got the innkeeper to call the archbishop's assistant, who said the meeting would be at eleven in a side room of the inn. Too keyed up to rest her fatigued body, Hollis went outside and walked. Three hours later she arrived at the empty room and laid her quilt on a table. She circled the table, rolled the quilt up, and then unrolled it again. She repeated the sequence twice, ultimately not leaving *Jimmy Carter* unfurled. 11:07 a.m. 11:08, 11:09.

At 11:10 the archbishop entered, saying he didn't know where they were supposed to meet and his assistant had left. Hollis often perceives others' emotions, and she felt apprehension and trouble from him. But then they sat down at a small square table, and he asked in a kind voice, "Are you cold? Are you warm? Would you like a drink of water?" Her body relaxing, Hollis felt like she was the great leader's first concern at that moment.

He began the meeting by praying for the world and for Hollis. Then he asked why she wanted to meet with him, and Hollis related her dream. She told him that when she lived in Western Africa—where realistic art is not part of the culture—she and a friend went into a village in Benin to draw people. She heard locals exclaiming to one another, "Look, the two white women can make photographs come from their fingers." On the following four days they drew increasingly bigger crowds of people who would stand behind and watch the drawing. The children imitated the drawing motion with their hands, lifting their eyes as Hollis did to observe and measure the lines she was making on the pages.

"I don't know the South African culture," she told him. "Before I do a larger-than-life purple image of you, I'd like to pass it by you first to get your blessing."

Archbishop Tutu put his head in his hands and then passed his hands over his hair and back again. "I know what you mean," he said. "They made a statue of me in Johannesburg. I went to the inauguration. When it was unveiled, I was there ... but I was here. It was very odd. So I thank you for asking, but," his voice became gentler, "I think this is okay."

Surprising Hollis with comments indicating some familiarity with her work, he asked to see what she'd brought. In her portfolio, he ran his fingers around the faces of people as he asked her practical questions, like whether she could make a living as an artist. Then she showed him *Jimmy Carter*.

While they were still seated at the table, the archbishop's assistant entered the room and said it was time to go. The archbishop again put his head in his hands and ran his fingers over his hair. Standing to leave, the archbishop said of President Carter, "He is truly one of the last remaining statesmen in America, and America will only appreciate how respected he is worldwide when he's no longer with us." And then he explained—dumbfounding Hollis—that his wife broke her toe just before the interview and that he'd come to meet with Hollis while his wife was waiting to go to the emergency room. "It's now time for me to be a devoted husband," he said, taking his leave. He was due to speak at the commencement at two o'clock.

It didn't rain. Hollis was able to sit in the audience with Alina and hear the archbishop praise the college. Berea was the South's first interracial and coeducational college. It admits only academically promising students, primarily from Appalachia, most with limited economic resources, and it charges no tuition. Coming from every US state and more than sixty other countries, the students represent a rich diversity of colors, cultures, and faiths. The college's inclusive Christian character is expressed in its motto, "God has made of one blood all peoples of the Earth." Obviously Berea's credo echoes that of Hollis and Archbishop Desmond Tutu.

Among the students processing with the graduating class, there was a man who'd come out of a refugee camp in Sudan and who would be going to teach at a school in Johannesburg, and there was a woman from Kenya who was going on to an Ivy League graduate program. Tears rolling down her checks, Hollis realized her fragile emotional state. She'd admired the world leader, but she was touched by a simple man meeting and showing kindness to a stranger making a piece of art about him when his wife had just suffered an injury. And now, that Sunday afternoon on the stage as he was speaking publicly, she saw his aura—a broad white light with pink touches surrounding him. It seemed like he was projecting a voice from elsewhere—another realm perhaps. He was funny, enlightening, and truthful. Hollis felt he shocked the audience when he went from the general call to love and forgive one's enemies to an exhortation for everyone to love and forgive all of their enemies, including Osama bin Laden, Saddam Hussein, and George W. Bush. The wonder of his address brought the assembly to silence.

Hollis welcomed these comments that May 2005. In her part of the country she thought no one was saying anything critical against the war in Iraq for fear of being labeled unpatriotic. (My, how far the San Francisco Bay Area is from North Carolina.)

I called Hollis the next summer when I was visiting family in Raleigh. She drove thirty minutes each way to bring me to her house for dinner with Reynald (whom I'd met in Santa Barbara) and their son Gaël, who was home for a few days before departing for a motorcycle trip through West Africa. Hollis had shown our classes photos of her home, family, and pets. Now her life came alive to me, turning from the country road into her drive lined with scrap metal sculptures, seeing the mass of potted plants on the front porch and the birdbaths and bird feeders placed for optimal viewing from the poolside table. Outside the dogs bounded over and nuzzled me. Inside her African parrot spoke his greeting in French and English. The visit was impromptu, so Hollis scrounged through her refrigerator, and with her natural culinary talent, she concocted a lip-smacking dinner of leftovers and organic produce.

In her studio the twelve feet by twelve feet flat working surface held two Berninas and a laptop. I couldn't wait to see how she organized the hundreds of threads she might use in the course of a day or two. (She'd told our machine quilting classes she often changes her top thread 250 times a day—that's why she uses monofilament in her bobbins.) In the studio's anteroom she had a fifty-inch-wide cabinet of shallow drawers that held all her Superior threads arranged in color and numerical sequence. But right next to her quilting spot she had a three-drawer Elfa cabinet—one drawer for warm colors, one for cool colors, and the bottom drawer for neutrals.

The highlight, of course, was her design wall, which was layered with her work. On the outer surface she'd pinned some small abstract pieces as well as a Toureg piece in process, but underneath—with all these pins holding up other work—was the not quite finished *Hope for Our World*. I was stunned that such a masterpiece would be covered with other work, but taking down the abstract pieces so I could experience the full impact of the piece behind, Hollis said, "Why not? It's just fabric and batting, and these are just pins." Larger than life, Archbishop Desmond Tutu was surrounded by the children of the world, including Hollis's own children at ages unrelated to their chronological years.

Reap As You Sew

Copyright 2007 by Hollis Chatelain, *Hope for Our World* (82" x 82")

"Nadia, Gaël, and Karen had to be in this scene because they are part of our world and the future. I've put my children here because we all need to take less so our children can have more, and we need them to also ask what they can do for the world," she said.

The thread work astounded me, especially because I could compare finished areas to areas not yet quilted (see page 41). I asked if I could touch the quilt, and I then lightly ran my hands over some of the faces, perhaps the way Archbishop Tutu had the day he saw *Jimmy Carter*. Hollis pointed out the many doves symbolizing world peace. I thought also of the peace that surpasses all understanding, spiritual peace, which is said to descend like a dove … or God's gift of the Spirit to individuals, also symbolized by a dove. With my eyes fixed on the quilt, Spirit started me singing to myself the song I first heard during the Gulf War, a song that always brings me to the verge of tears.

Let there be peace on earth
and let it begin with me.
Let there be peace on earth,
the peace that was meant to be.
With God as our Father,
brothers all are we.
Let me walk with my brother
in perfect harmony.

(LET THERE BE PEACE ON EARTH
By Sy Miller and Jill Jackson
Copyright © 1955, Renewed 1983, by Jan-Lee Music (ASCAP)
International Copyright Secured. All Rights Reserved. Reprinted by permission.)

Aftermath and Healing

Two years later Hollis and I sat in my California family room an hour before the workshop participants arrived for our 2008 workshop. I was formally interviewing her for this book—an odd feeling since we've shared so many informal one-on-one conversations during meals, late nights, airport runs, and an Empty Spools session at Asilomar. I felt nervous as well as amazed that Hollis seemed flattered. She'd been interviewed dozens of times, and this was my first book. I remain embarrassingly ignorant about Africa, and I'm not a social activist. Yet I sense that she respects me because even when we envision different means, we value the same ends. We respect each other's experiences and often seek input from each other. And we're both women of passion.

Rehashing the story of *Hope for Our World*, Hollis told me she'd had an intuition. She'd opened her heart, received and honored the dream, and identified her need and her desire, and then the Berea invitation appeared. When the invitation to Berea came to her unsolicited—except spiritually—she knew she would meet the great man. I had no doubt that was true. In fact, during all the recounting of the obstacles, it seemed obvious that she would, of course, meet him. I'm sure you sensed it too, reading this.

What may be more surprising is that the meeting and the archbishop's prayer for Hollis bore delicious fruit. Beforehand Hollis had agonizing stage fright. Her chosen career required her to speak before public audiences, and she would go days without sleep before an appearance. Even if all she had to do was spend five or ten minutes introducing herself and her work at an after-dinner Asilomar gathering, she'd tell her students all day how apprehensive she was, and she'd ask them to come and sit where she could focus on their familiar faces. After her meeting with Archbishop Tutu she was healed of her fear of public speaking almost completely. At the Sisters Quilt Show in Oregon, Hollis's first appearance after her encounter with Archbishop Tutu, she addressed the largest audience she'd ever had. She was comfortable, and the crowd of 850 gave her a standing ovation.

Whereas before the meeting she'd felt stuck in the design phase, afterward the drawings for the purple quilt came to her easily. "I felt happy and peaceful working on the piece," she told me. "I actually felt the love emanating from Archbishop Tutu." She flowed smoothly through the technical difficulties without the jarring tension that working through the biggest quilting challenges used to stir up.

She had less attachment to *Precious Water* when it came time to sell it.

But she had a new attachment of sorts—if you can call commitment to a passionate cause an attachment. When she finished and exhibited *Hope for Our World*, people felt they could walk up to it and feel something extra. "It needs to go out," they would tell her. So Hollis and Reynald put together a traveling exhibit called *Imagine Hope*. The first venue was Duke University, where ten of Hollis's monochromatically dye-painted and lavishly quilted "statement pieces" promoting social change were exhibited along with complementary photographs by other artists. With content about resources and the environment, education, political and economic refugees, fair trade, children of the world, and peace, Hollis longed for this collection to move people to actively participate in making beneficial changes. She envisioned the exhibit traveling to many venues where local organizations dealing with the subject matter of her art would be on hand to educate the public and facilitate their participation for change. And it did travel to other important venues—Berea College, the National Quilt Museum, and the International Quilt Festival in both Houston and Long Beach. But having ten large intricate pieces in a traveling exhibit limited her ability to sell them, some of which had taken her years to complete. Others were already sold and available on loan for just a short time. Although Hollis was willing to put her family's livelihood, her talent, her heart, and her soul on the line to serve the causes for which she was passionate, when the economic crisis hit, there weren't enough willing corporate sponsors and wealthy underwriters. The words *hope* and *change* had taken on a divisive connotation that some potential venues feared. And the varied ownership of the quilts posed unresolvable insurance and timing issues.

When Hollis opened her heart, received and honored the dream, and identified her need to meet Archbishop Tutu, she met him against all odds. I invite everyone touched by Hollis's dedication to have faith and to join in the intention that her work and ours will come to the ends for which the work is created. Encouraging awareness and social activism through art is Hollis's life purpose. I believe that when anyone is living to fulfill a genuine calling, the universe—and that includes individuals—honors what is sacred by supporting that intention. May it be so with Hollis, with me, and with you.

--- STEPS ALONG A SPIRITUAL QUILTMAKING PATH ---

CONSIDER WHAT YOUR SPIRITUALITY MEANS TO YOU AND HOW YOU LIVE YOUR LIFE. Living a purposeful life according to your spiritual beliefs and higher purpose gives you the satisfaction of having meaning, simplifies and focuses your life, motivates you, and according to many religions, brings you eternal life or a better life next time.

ACT: Pray or set an intention to become more aware of the answers to the following questions, asking yourself the questions repeatedly and letting the responses percolate in your subconscious for a while so that you can learn or confirm your highest calling. Or ask Spirit to clarify your special calling directly.

ASK & JOURNAL:
- When do you feel most exhilarated? When do you feel you are being most uniquely special? What did you especially enjoy as a child? What about you elicited the most praise from other people? What do you dream about that brings you joy?
- Once you know your calling, ask yourself some questions. Is how you spend your time consistent with what you've identified as your highest calling or life purpose? If it is, kudos! To give more time to activities in line with your calling, ask yourself regularly if there are small steps you can take to make it more fun, more efficient, or a higher priority?

ACT: If, after trying to uncover the answer, you aren't sure what your purpose or calling is, consider working with a trusted counselor, a life or creativity coach, or a good spiritual director or coach to help you figure it out. Don't know how to find someone to help you? Spiritual Directors International is one source for spiritual directors throughout the US and across many spiritual traditions and outlooks, and many of its members also do dream work (check out sdiworld.org/seek-and-find). My own spiritual director training was through the Monastery of the Risen Christ School for Charismatic Spiritual Directors. Kaizen-Muse Creativity Coaching™ (www.kaizenmuse.com/coaches/) is a good resource for certified creativity coaches. Ericka Jackson and The Kingdom Ministers Training Institute™ offer in-depth certification programs for Convergence coaches whose purpose is to lead and guide Christians in fulfilling their callings (www.convergence-coach.com). They also train Spiritual Cleansing Specialists to help bring Christians to greater freedom and healthier mindsets (www.spiritualcleansingspecialist.com). My personal experiences and training in these four approaches have influenced this book and are incorporated into Reap As You Sew™ retreats and my one-on-one client work.

***

CONSIDER WHAT YOU NEED TO MAKE PURSUING YOUR CREATIVE DREAM MORE FULFILLING OR EASIER: Returning to the United States to turn textile art into her family's livelihood, Hollis decided that a next step was to improve her sewing skills and learn piecing. She identified that the person she'd like to learn from was Caryl Bryer Fallert (now Fallert-Gentry). She took the first step of writing Caryl a letter to ask for her help. Not long afterwards she got together with Caryl and learned the desired sewing skills from that expert!

ASK & JOURNAL:
- Are there other avenues you'd like to explore with your quiltmaking?
- Is there a class you'd like to take or a new technique you'd like to explore?

ACT:
- First brainstorm. And when you're ready, set five-year, one-year and short-term goals. Some of you may wish to ask Spirit to help you with this. Goals don't have to be completions and countable, but there should be a way of knowing if you've done what you set out to do.
- Commit the goals to writing. Or if you're more visual, create a vision board of images. Assign a target date by which to start taking steps to achieve each goal. Having specific goals vastly increases chances of reaching them! And try to set reasonable expectations!
- For the short-term goal, identify a next action or a first step—one that's not too big (so you won't be afraid about having to leap) and one that's definitely possible to complete soon.
- Make a note in your calendar or time management system to take the first step.
- Now take that step!
- Identify and calendar next steps each time you've completed the previous step.
- Review whether you're achieving or approaching your goals at least quarterly, and revise them if you wish. After all, they are yours!

EXAMPLE: Let's say you're a quilter and your goal is to help women live full lives uninhibited by societal emphasis on external beauty, sexiness, and youthfulness. So you write, "<u>Five years from now</u>: my style incorporates humor to get women thinking about ages and stages of life, and I teach fun quilt workshops centered on this theme three times a year. <u>One year from now</u>: I've made at least two humorous quilts (of any size) about menopause marking the entry into a joyful and wise time of a woman's life, and I'll enter at least one into a local show. <u>Next summer</u>: I'll design a wallhanging about giving up the notion of having a model's body type. <u>This month</u>: I'll start an idea folder.

* * *

CONSIDER THE BENEFITS OF PRACTICE. Hollis sees her talent as giftedness enhanced by practice, hard work, and patience. Like the rest of us, she makes mistakes she rips out. I've heard her say more than once in response to expressed awe over how good her machine quilting is, "Well, I think if you do something hours a day almost every day and you don't get good at it, you've probably chosen the wrong pursuit!" Beginners almost always need practice, and so do intermediates on their way to becoming masters. Even those at the top of a profession often try to improve, innovate, or branch out. Remember, while practice doesn't make us perfect, it can make us pretty darn good (Jill Badonsky, *The Nine Modern Day Muses (And a Bodyguard): Ten Guides to Creative Inspiration,* Renegade Muses Publishing House, 2010, p. 152). You might also enjoy reading Jill's *The Muse Is In: An Owner's Manual to Your Creativity* (Running Press, 2013).

ASK & JOURNAL: Is there something you want to improve? Are you putting in the time to develop your gift? Give yourself a break if you're not meeting the high standards you expect of yourself. Enjoy the process. And if you'd like to improve, why not put in some practice?

ACT:
- Read the Reap As You Sew blog post on "The Beauty of Imperfection," www.reapasyousew.com/2013/10/26/the-beauty-of-imperfection/.
- Make a charity quilt as a vehicle for practicing machine quilting or whatever skill you previously identified as something you'd like to improve. The recipients will be touched by the unexpected gift and your generous donation of time and materials. They will not be disparaging your stitches or criticizing your design.
- Make some quilt sandwiches out of two layers of cotton and your usual batting (or experiment with different fabrics or battings, marking on the sample which batting is inside so that you can later compare the looks). Whenever you're going to start machine quilting for the day, or when you're about to change from one type of quilting to another (such as from zigzags to circles), stitch first on one of these sandwiches, awakening muscle memory, experimenting with size or curves, balancing thread and bobbin tension, etc. Tennis pros don't go out and start playing without a warm-up. Why should quilters?

* * *

CONSIDER THE BEST WAYS TO GET YOURSELF TO SHOW UP FOR YOUR CREATIVE WORK.

ASK & IMAGINE:
- Do you do best by working steadily in regular increments or in sporadic bursts? In small chunks of time or in hours or days on end? The answer may depend on or influence where your work area is, as well as other demands on your time. If spurts are your M.O., is this adequate?
- Now ask yourself if there are any changes you might try that would bring you more fun or more productive time? Post a reminder on your nightstand and every day for a week, take one minute and just sit and daydream about what a fabulously creative life and setting would look like for you. There are many good answers! Maybe clues will even come to you in your dreams if you think about this just before you go to sleep.
- How about taking a month and trying a different approach if you don't already have a satisfying situation of time and place to create what wants to be created?

SHARE: I'd love to have you e-mail chris@reapasyousew.com about anything that touched you deeply from following any of the suggestions in this chapter.

Over Zen: Sue's "Only Don't Know" Approach

Barely acquainted, Suzan Friedland and I sat cross-legged on floor cushions in her apartment near Laurel Village in San Francisco. I'd come to interview her that chilly October morning in 2008, but I sensed that we should meditate before we talked. Her windows were open, so she offered me her new *Over Zen* quilt to throw over my shoulders. Afterward we'd talk about her making that quilt, so I accepted it, interested in enveloping myself in its energy.

She tapped her chime, and we began in silence, focused on our breathing. I was accustomed to allowing thoughts to pass by, and as usual, thoughts did come and go. *This is so cool. I'm in my centering prayer, sitting in silent meditation with a Buddhist. What a great beginning for an interview.* Then ... quiet ... timeless being in the stillness ... until vrooommm, vrooommm, and a thunderous *vrooommm. Is a war starting?* I wondered. *This is deafening and close! Oh, ignore it. Let awareness of these sounds and your thoughts about them pass. Repeat your sacred word*, I told myself. *Ab-ba, Ab-ba*. Though work is the antithesis of meditation, I labored at emptying my mind. When the ending chime sounded, I was relieved.

"Wow!" I said to Sue. "Could you ignore that? What was it?"

"Oh, I forgot. It's Fleet Week. The US Navy's Blue Angels are in town for their annual air show. Squadrons of fighter jets in formation. Right over the city and the Golden Gate Bridge. Hard to ignore." We laughed.

Before I met Sue, I researched and found that 20 to 30 million Americans quilted. Furthermore, nine out of ten American adults believed in God, a universal spirit, or a higher power, and 85 percent of Americans called themselves Christians. The Pew Forum on Religion & Public Life has since updated its report to show that 78 percent of American adults self-identified as Christians. 5 percent belonged to non-Christian religions, and 6 percent were unaffiliated with any particular religion (religions.pewforum.org/pdf/report-religious-landscape-study-full.pdf.) So when I began work on this book, I ballparked that there were close to twenty million Christian quilters in the United States; however, I underestimated the sociological preference for spirituality over religiosity. A later *Washington Post* poll reported that 70 percent of those affiliated with a religion believe that many religions or belief systems can lead to eternal salvation and 75 percent believed their own religion's teachings are open to interpretation (Jacqueline L. Salmon, "Most Americans Believe in Higher Power, Poll Finds," *Washington Post*, June 24, 2008.) In short, most Americans are not rigid believers.

I got a taste of these attitudes at a writer's conference in Guatemala in the summer of 2008, and soon afterward—with Spirit's guidance—I revamped my book's menu of stories to serve up not only Christian dishes but more of a smorgasbord. I didn't dream of the dessert to follow—that shortly afterward I'd lead spiritual quilting retreats with a Zen Buddhist, be in a close-knit group with a theosophist, travel to Mexico to quilt our dreams with a minister of Spiritual Peacemaking, and work with a mystical Jewish editor—all of whom I'd treasure as friends.

Spiritual women long to connect with others at a level far deeper than work, social contexts, and even quilt guilds typically foster. When I sought non-Christian spiritual quilters to interview, the first of many to contact me was Suzan Friedland, an accomplished Zen Buddhist textile artist. She sounded as excited to talk to me as I was to get a response from her. On the surface, it might have seemed unlikely that an analytical, Catholic, ex-lawyer trying to find her own niche in quiltmaking and a bouncy, spontaneous, Zen Buddhist textile artist with a signature style would end up collaborating on running spiritual retreats. Yet our first face-to-face meeting might have been a clue. At Sue's impromptu invitation I stopped by Sue's Gualala, CA home one evening, where she and five of her quilting friends were enjoying a weekend getaway. We toured her studio, and I saw *Over Zen* and much of her other work. We decided to feature

Chris Boersma Smith

Over Zen in this book, and we set up the October interview in San Francisco. I ended up staying for one of Sue-the-chef's vegetarian feasts.

Suzan Friedland in her Gualala yard

Before the interview, I read up on Buddhism, which I'd only studied in world religion survey courses. I was reminded that Buddhism is not a religion as much as a prescription for living, embracing four tenets briefly stated as follows: (1) essentially impermanent, all life is suffering; (2) attachment or desire causes suffering; (3) once Nirvana or enlightenment is reached suffering ceases; and (4) there is a path that leads out of suffering to enlightenment. Buddhism permeates Sue's life the way all faiths probably ought to, the way mystical experience or life-changing encounters with the sacred often do. Sue was raised as a Catholic and saw herself as a freethinker by age 10 or 11, when art captivated her. When she was very young and living in the Bay Area, her mother took her to museums weekly. She finger-painted at the Museum of Modern Art, but the Asian Art Museum was Sue's favorite. Its influence shows up in her current work. Both Catholicism and school seemed too structured for Sue. She was (in her own words) visual, dyslexic, and scatterbrained, so she wrapped herself up in her art.

For fifteen years before she went for her master's degree in fine arts, Sue worked in creative fields, primarily as a chef in the hotel and restaurant business and as a theatrical lighting designer. Along the way she met and married Karl, who'd studied Buddhism since high school. She saw him meditating and studying the Pali Text Society's *Discourses of the Buddha*. She sat in on intellectual studies. Then despite her difficulty reading, she took a class at San Francisco State to learn the history of Zen Buddhism, and she spent hours with Karl's volumes on the subject.

Distilling what she learned down to the four noble truths and the notion that the temple is inside, Sue came to what worked for her: (1) keeping her heart open to receive and (2) practicing nonattachment, simplicity, and meditation. "Spirituality is an inner intuition," Sue says. "I've always felt I had a gift within that kept me going through life's ups and downs. Pursuing it, I don't have to tell anyone or pray to anyone. I don't need to explain it. Some can do that with words, but for me it comes out in art." Sue and Karl have now been married for more than twenty-five years, and their lives reflect their Zen Buddhism from their homes' clean décor, Karl's dedication to the Japanese Shakuhachi bamboo flute, and their vegan diet and green tea to Sue's art and easygoing nature.

In 1986, Sue began working in textiles after attending a quilt show and being attracted to the quilts' textural qualities much like she'd been attracted to the energy of huge Jackson Pollack canvases when she and her mother visited art museums in the sixties. Even now her work is not about pattern or color. Like most good art, Sue's work expresses her own feelings. It presents surfaces manipulated with detail work until viewers can feel the texture without touching and have their emotions stirred just by walking in and looking without analyzing.

Indeed, one collector of Sue's work is an artist with degenerative retinal disease, and it's the texture of Sue's textile art that captivates her!

Copyright 1995 by Suzan Friedland, *Zoetic* (86"x66") featured in Robert Shaw's book, *The Art Quilt* (Hugh Lauter Levin Associates, 1997). Made with living hemp and linen, *Zoetic* reflects Sue's take on the theme of living, specifically that quilting brings her to life.

Meditation and quiltmaking grounded Sue during the years when she was taking care of her dying parents. "I would've run around chaotically or aimlessly—in today's world we might say I'd have been psycho—if it weren't for my spirituality. Meditation and art are one for me. They slow me down enough so I can think of what I need to do. Walking three to five miles every morning in the Presidio or up in Gualala in the woods or along the beach—that's meditative and grounding for me too. I observe texture while I walk, and my observations evoke strong feelings. My Zen practice makes me very aware of the paradox of trying to capture the changing elements I observe, so I gravitate toward trying to capture ephemeral qualities like a dying branch, the colors of fading flowers, and the texture of clouds. I am so blessed to have the gift of art and the practice of meditation. They bring me peace. I'll do art and meditation my whole life."

Interestingly in Zen Buddhism enlightenment through meditation often uses paradoxical statements to transcend rational thought. When I saw Sue's long résumé, another paradox aroused my curiosity. I asked how she squares nonattachment with a creative life that thrives on recognition and acclaim to exhibit in galleries, compete for limited artist-in-residence programs, and support oneself financially through art. Her mixed media pieces have appeared in numerous publications and exhibits (including *Visions* and *Quilt National*). She earned a Vermont Studio Center full-fellowship residency. She has lectured and taught on surface design, and she's participated in annual open-studio tours that seek to promote sales of the artists' works.

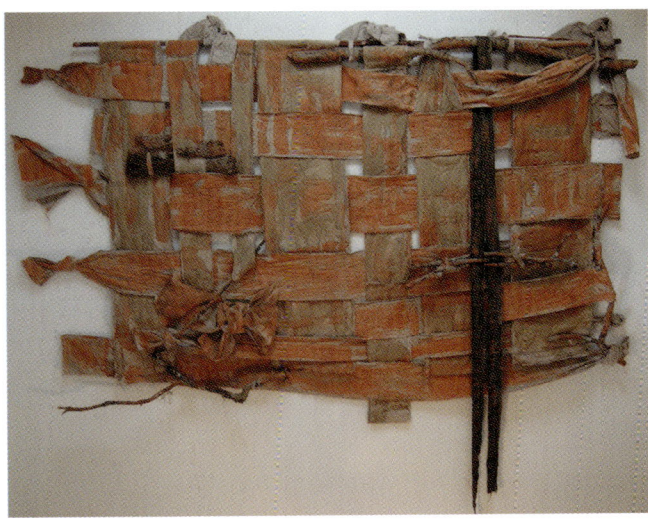

Copyright 2007 by Suzan Friedland, *Gift of Time* (84" x 36")

"You do what you do, and people will come to you. As for open studios, if they come, they come. I do what I need to do to get my emotions out, to survive in the world, but I have no attachment to the pieces. I want them out. I want them to evoke emotion in other people. I give some of my work away, but when I price it, I put big prices on quality work." She paused, looked away, and then continued. "As an artist making a living from art, there's a dilemma. Only rich people can afford art. Last year during the studio tour 400 people saw

Chris Boersma Smith

my work and the environment I created to exhibit in. Sharing my art with so many people excited me much more than the two sales I made at high prices. I treat all visitors with the same respect, and I love to hear their stories—what the pieces remind them of. One piece touched a woman whose son had just died. With one of my quilts, she felt his presence. The piece resonated with her, and now it's hers."

Sue's body of work is extensive, so I wanted to know how she produces it, and the answer surprised me. She works in spurts. She says series percolate during times when she's not able to produce art. Sue has her own style characterized by simplicity and the use of neutrals, but "it would be dull," she says, "not to keep trying different things. It's fun to see yourself evolve." She always finishes one series before she moves on to the next.

This series of photos shows Sue's creative process from start to finish:

Starting with linen panels . . .

Sue made her first brushstrokes on the linen.

She kept adding marks

And layers made it more complex.

Then it was basted for quilting.

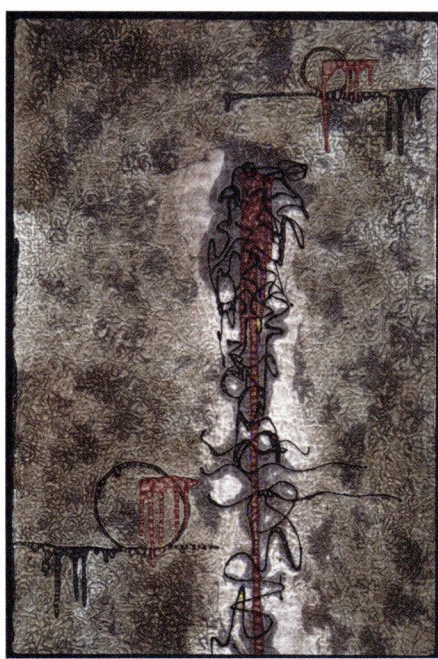

The details are exquisite.

And here it is finished!
Copyright 1998 by Suzan Friedland, *Green Tea* (144" x 121")

Each series may involve a technique or certain fabric or other material (such as recycled materials for her mixed-media art). She gets her fabric by the bolt—natural Czechoslovakian linen or Pendleton wool or prepared-for-dyeing muslin. She usually has ideas and processes for a series developing in her head for six to twelve months. The actual production is much faster. Her wool throw series was one she thought about for a year after a friend who lives near Pendleton, Oregon, gave her some wool scraps at their annual Point Bonita quilt camp. She decided to use the wool and make a series of Japanese brush-painted monoprints with free-flowing quilting. Big enough to curl up in, the pieces would have soft organic flannel backs.

Then for pieces within the series, she may start with something observed on a walk, like the huge boulders at Bowling Ball Beach on the Mendocino coast, or with a feeling like anger or with a title like *Over Zen*. She thinks of titles first, then process, and only later begins the physical creation.

For example, with *Over Zen*, she considered two meanings for the phrase. First she thought of her intent of quilting all over the surface, of being in a Zen meditative mode while stitching. Secondly she thought of how people overuse the word *Zen* and how she's sick of hearing that. Googling "Zen moment" yields almost 10 million hits in less than a half second, with the top definition saying it relates to waking up to the present moment without the filter of ideas and opinions. Even my asking questions about this quilt took something away. Sue never really wants to explain her pieces because she wants viewers to bring their own imaginations to the title, devoid of the artist's ideas and opinions.

After titles Sue thinks about process. Usually she works it all out in her head before she begins her work, although sometimes, she says, you must be spontaneous because you can't foresee or plan for everything. For *Over Zen*, she laid out huge sheets of plastic to make a monoprint. She brushed paint onto the plastic and then laid the wool on top. The paint wasn't soaking in. So she came up with the idea of using her body as a brayer. Like a kid on a lawn, she rolled her whole body across the fabric, back and forth, and that was it! Ironically her body gave the title a third meaning, as she was literally *over* (on top of) *Zen* in the making of it.

Chris Boersma Smith

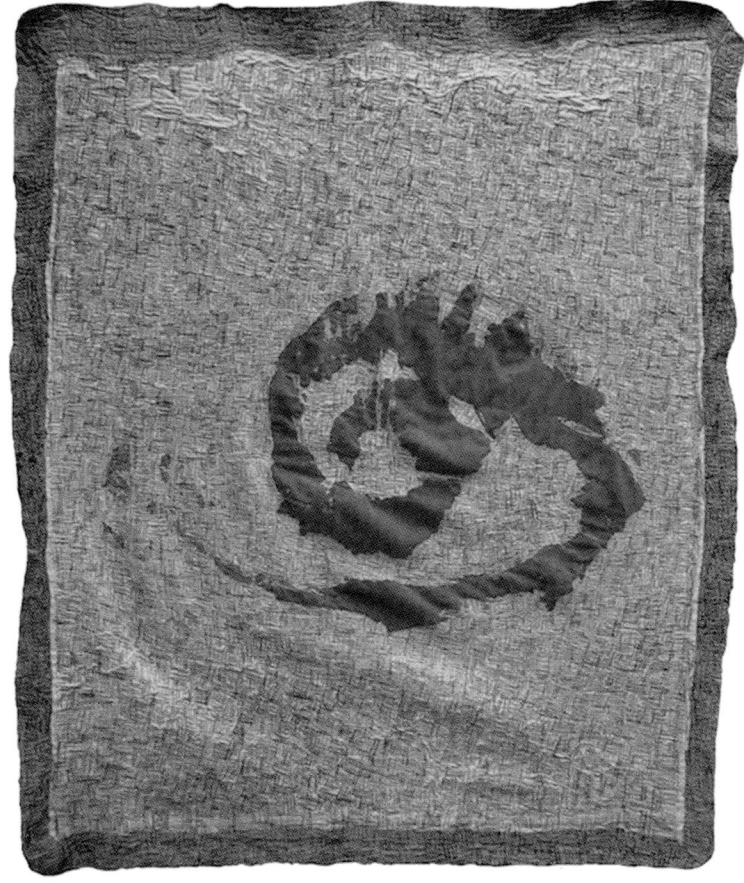

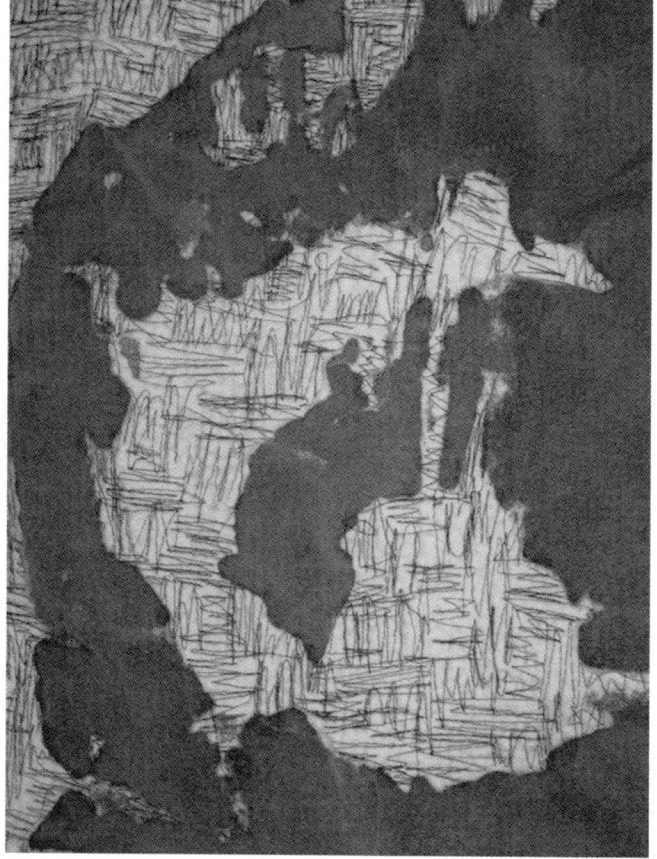

Copyright 2008 by Suzan Friedland, *Over Zen* (55" x 68") (full and detail)

While watching Sue paint is intriguing, watching her quilt is *mesmerizing*. She sets herself up with a stack of fifteen prewound bobbins because she puts miles of thread on a piece. She likes to quilt in complete silence—no music. When she's quilting in the zone, she doesn't want to stop and break her rhythm when one bobbin runs out. If need be, she'll grab a bobbin wound with a different (albeit neutral) color rather than stop to wind a bobbin.

She uses an industrial Bernina at a speed that nearly breaks the sound barrier. Of course, nothing is marked. She may have a few straight pins folding the back onto the front to create an edge treatment, and she may sew a few pins right into the quilt because she's moving too fast to get them out. Often with black or neutral threads, she produces a pattern of repeating spirals or crisscrosses or some other design that seems to come out of her fingers without having passed through an analytic brain cell at all. She goes for *inconsistent consistency*, like leaving some selvage but not all or quilting some design but varying the shapes and placement or throwing in some other designs as well.

When the series is done, its end is as apparent to Sue as the T-intersection at the end of a country lane. It's time to turn in another direction.

She may not always be producing, but whether she is awake, asleep, or unable to sleep, Sue is constantly designing. The next opportunity I had to sit with Sue came when we spent a week in Mexico doing a quilt retreat, meditating together, learning some new painting, design, and quilting techniques that she taught. But the most fascinating part was just being with her. Even when she's dealing with everyday life, she's an artist. She's a chef who delights as much in the presentation as in the tastes and the creativity of taking local ingredients and turning them into a masterpiece. And she cooks at our retreats just for the fun of it!

Breakfast by Sue at a Reap As You Sew retreat in Baja

Inspiration for texture comes to Sue from seeing things like this on a morning walk in San José del Cabo

Sue's a keen and enthusiastic observer. We walked through a botanical cactus garden, and she focused on the spikes and the scars on the succulents, where the texture was most unusual. She mentally collected all these textures as potential design ideas. I, on the other hand, kept shooting photos, hoping to have something to work from later. In falling-down bricks leaving exposed mortar, she saw inspiration rather than dilapidation.

She enjoyed grace before meals and yoga and selecting local pottery as a gift for her niece. She rejoiced in the sunsets, the moonrises, the bubbles in the Jacuzzi, the fireworks, and even the gust of wind that tipped over a container of paint onto a painted fabric that was sitting out to dry because it had been deemed finished. It just had another layer, and layers are good! Here's another paradox: because of Sue's grounding in her spirituality, the spirit of this bundle of energy is free to ascend like the Blue Angels.

--- STEPS ALONG A SPIRITUAL QUILTMAKING PATH ---

CONSIDER INTENTIONALLY ESTABLISHING A REGULAR SPIRITUAL CREATIVE PROCESS. Especially in our society that values productivity so highly, quiet time and sacred self-care time are often missing. Common thinking is that meditation, journaling, prayer, walking, yoga, and/or exercise should be done first thing in the morning, but that doesn't work well for everyone, particularly if you engage in more than one of those.

EXAMPLES:
- Sue sits on a cushion for morning meditation after coffee and email, but on an empty stomach. She often takes a long morning walk to observe colors and textures, and that's her pre-creativity meditation on those days. She doesn't photograph the textures she sees, but she keenly observes them.
- A creativity coaching client of mine recently discovered that her ego doesn't really wake up until ten in the morning, though she usually gets up much earlier. So now she enjoys creativity time before ten o'clock and creates more freely.

ASK & JOURNAL: What's worked for you before and/or what would be an easy way for you to carve out some quiet time and/or sacred self-care time? What would be a first small step to start (or to revitalize) a practice that refills your well? Once you have an answer or a first small step, do it and keep an open mind. (Inspired by Jill Badonsky, co-founder of the Kaizen-Muse Creativity Coaching™ method, www.kaizenmusecreativitycoaching.com, and Ericka Jackson, founder of the Convergence Coaching™ method, www.convergence-coach.com.)

***

CONSIDER SETTING UP YOUR CREATIVE PROJECTS AHEAD SO YOU CAN BEGIN RIGHT AFTER MEDITATION OR CENTERING.

STEPS FOR PREPARING TO CREATE:
- If painting, protect your work surface, select fabric, and cut it. Get out paints, your apron, brushes, cups, wipe-up cloths, and a tub or jug of water.
- If sewing, de-clutter your work area, oil your machine and wind bobbins, and set up the cutting board, iron, design wall, whatever you'll need.
- If your projects go on for days or longer, try to have a place or maybe a portable board on which you can keep the project materials ready, even if you can only work for fifteen minutes at a time.

***

CONSIDER SETTING THE TONE FOR THE DAY THROUGH THESE ACTION STEPS:
- Write down an intention or guiding word in the morning. In *Art Is a Spiritual Path* (Shambhala 2005), Pat Allen urges writing down a present tense, specific intention as if it is an already answered prayer—without using want which implies not having—and then forgetting about it as you create. Other people ask Spirit for a guiding word for the day (like play, rejoice, calm, light). Their inner being hears and responds accordingly.
- Create during the day.
- Afterwards, reflect back and journal about how the intention or guiding word manifested.

CONSIDER HOW YOUR ART IS INFLUENCED BY YOUR SENSES AND YOUR EMOTIONS.
What we hear while we are creating can reverberate in us, affecting different quilters in different ways and affecting the same person differently during various parts of the creative process.

EXAMPLES: In a Kaffe Fassett workshop, I found that his selection of sixties vocals led me to select happy and bright colors, and I sang and danced as my right brain placed fabrics intuitively on my design board. I created this book's cover quilt design with lots of curved and flowing lines while listening to a sensuous Brazilian vocalist whom I knew would bring out my inner bossa nova dancer. In workshop settings, I cannot design while chatter is happening around me, so I often bring earplugs and my iTunes; however, I've seen that for others, conversation engages their left brain, leaving the right brain to create without the analyst jumping in.

ACT: Experiment with what works best for you. Silence or music? If music, then what kind? African drums, strings, piano? Vocals in a foreign language, Gregorian chants, ocean sounds, classical or New Age Bach? Maybe silence for some tasks like painting, and a flowing instrumental like the theme from *Out of Africa* for quilting? Observe how sound affects you, and then use sounds or silence to your advantage.

* * *

CONSIDER FREEING YOURSELF TO CREATE FROM YOUR INNATE KNOWING. Especially when you're painting on fabric, inside you have a feel for what you really want to express or how you want to play. We often overthink our art. There's a time for standing back and critiquing our compositions and design choices, but that's like editing and spell-checking. Save it for later.

PROJECT—PRACTICE CREATIVE FREEDOM BY DOING SOME TEXTILE PAINTING ON SMALL PIECES OF FABRIC. The materials investment is small. Cleanup is easy, and you're creating fabric rather than finished quilts, which helps silence the critic that laments wastefulness. Everything you create can be cut up, manipulated, painted over, and at worst, abandoned without feeling you've invested too much in it.

1. Get your materials:
   - Cotton or muslin, cut into half-yard or smaller pieces. Do not use prepared-for-dying (PFD) fabric, because PFD fabric has soda ash in it, which carries a fire risk if you put the fabric in the dryer without washing it first.
   - Setacolor fabric paints
   - Some tall heavy plastic cups or jars for mixing paint in
   - Any variety of paintbrushes or sponges
   - If water isn't nearby, have a tub of water or water in a large jug or pitcher.
   - Have an apron or old clothes and some paper towels and/or wipe up cloths handy.

2. Prepare to start:
   - Cover your work surface with plastic. (This could even be outside on the ground.)
   - Select cut fabric.
   - Set out your available or chosen paint colors.
   - Set out your apron, brushes, wipe-up cloths, and water ahead of time.

3. Do something to quiet the inner critic/analytical left brain—like the practices described above—sitting or walking meditation, selecting certain music, or writing down a specific word of intention.

4. Paint the fabric:
   - Lay out fabric on the plastic-covered work surface (several pieces at a time if there is room).
   - Mix or pour out small amounts of some paint colors into cups and then highly dilute them with water.
   - Apply paint with brushes or sponges or even just pour it on. This is an abstract so don't worry about whether you "can paint" or not. Just have fun with the chosen colors or the mood or intention word. Let go. No worries. You can't do this wrong! You can layer on color after color, or you can let one color dry a while and then go back and paint on other colors. You won't know the results ahead of time because the properties of multiple colors on different fabrics applied with varied techniques are unpredictable. Also, some of the color will set or fade more than others.
   - At any point in the process or at the end, you can tumble your air-dried painted fabric in a dryer on a high setting to set the color. Afterwards, the fabric can be ironed or not.

5. Make a small quilt using some of the painted fabric.
   - Take some of the painted fabric and sandwich it into a quilt. You can crinkle and pin on different fabrics to make a composition, and you can turn the edges of the backing over to the front loosely to make a casually finished edge.
   - Then wind some bobbins and thread your machine. Before you begin, decide what to quilt—lots of spirals, giant stippling, jagged lines, or anything else that's not too fussy.
   - Jump in and quilt away with your free motion foot, hardly any planning, and no marking. Practice just being in the present moment while quilting. Again, no worries. Just let it go.
   - Look at what you've created. You may or may not like your finished product, but you will have had a chance to express something and to play in a carefree way. Ask yourself what parts of this process you enjoyed? Was there anything that you learned about yourself or your feelings while doing this? Does the quilt have a name? Or a message? Is there something about this that might inspire another project?

***

CONSIDER ACCEPTING THAT SOME OF WHAT YOU PRODUCE WON'T BE YOUR FINEST WORK.
However, it all can all be a learning opportunity, a fun exploration, and best of all, a potential breakthrough. Sue reminds others that one thing we can say for sure about life is that we "only don't know" what it holds. Likewise, when we begin a quilt or art piece, we "only don't know" how it will turn out.

ACT: Practice letting go of creative outcomes by starting with what you feel most certain about. For example, right now I want to explore the texture of a certain seashell, or right now I have an idea of how to quilt the lower left triangle. Perhaps start with a title. Follow that idea without concern about the overall outcome. Take it a step at a time. When is the piece finished? Perhaps when you "only don't know" anything more that the piece is calling you to do.

Like Making Pasta: A Mother-Daughter Healing Quilt

We were on different continents when Kacie called from college to see whether I was willing to collaborate with her on a mixed media art quilt. Toby and I were making a San Francisco connection at London's Heathrow Airport. His Blackberry rang, and he pulled it from his belt case. Back in her ninety-year-old walk-up near Washington University in St. Louis, our daughter was using her cell phone to offer me an olive branch. She'd speed-dialed her dad's number because she knew he'd answer a call from her, and she wasn't so sure I would.

Kacie didn't know that I'd spent the past hour on a flight from Paris reading *Strong Women, Soft Hearts: A Woman's Guide to Cultivating a Wise Heart and a Passionate Life*, a Christian self-help book by Paula Rinehart (Thomas Nelson, 2005). Partway through, I'd turned to Toby and said, "This book is perfect for me right now. The author talks about the paradox of being a woman—that is, we have strong desires and capacity for relationship but relationships defy our attempts at control, leaving us vulnerable to loss and pain."

Toby grinned, seeming to only hear the last part of what I said. "So are you admitting to trying to be in control?"

"I suppose." I didn't bite. "What really hits me is her idea that many women keep busy to avoid their pain the way I do. Trying to protect ourselves, we close off the door to our heart to avoid distress, but then the heart is locked inside and isn't free to pursue its passions. And as a result, she says, we live a smaller, sort of frozen-in-place life instead of the full life we were created for, the one we long for." I took a deep breath. "You know, I've been praying for seven months that Kacie and I can get beyond the hurt and anger between us. If we don't, this book says neither one of us will ever really be okay."

He nodded but didn't say anything because of how often he and I'd talked about ways for me to get along with Kacie. Besides, he wasn't yet convinced that prayer was a worthwhile use of time. I went back to reading in silence, once again dwelling on the unfairness of my having the problem with her when both he and I had triggered and participated in the fight that precipitated the giant chasm between her and me but not between her and him. Was that just because I'm her mother and he's her father, not personal at all? I wondered … or more accurately I hoped. Is it because he's characteristically stoic and solutions-oriented, whereas my heart shows on my face, even as I'm willing it not to, giving away what I'd rather keep to myself?

I'm a quilter, sometimes wound as tight as a bobbin. Kacie is a sensitive artist, a printmaking major. Toby and I have debated whether we should have focused less on giving her so much opportunity and more on teaching her to accept limits. But we both knew this: She and I hadn't had any conversation longer than "Hi, how's it going?" and "Fine" in the past seven months. Even before that, her going cross-country five years earlier to attend Philips Exeter Academy as a high school junior had started the rift between her and us that then kept widening.

The Teen Years Had Exacerbated Our Issues

Before Exeter when Toby, Kacie, her younger sister Brenna, and I sat around the dinner table, Kacie spoke of her day with endless detail and opinions … like how the soccer coach shouldn't only play Meghan as goalie but should let Devon tend goal sometimes because Devon was a senior and it wasn't fair and Meghan was full of herself anyway. Brenna would open her mouth to speak but not fast enough because Kacie would start again, telling how her art teacher selected two of Kacie's drawings for an exhibit at the library. At times Kacie and Brenna whispered and laughed together, but they also bickered as sisters two years apart often do. Clothing in the other's closet was a common trigger. Had the teal Dixie Chicks T-shirt been given or lent? Toby and I clung to the hope that although the separation would tear apart our family, having Kacie at Exeter might give Brenna a chance to get out of Kacie's shadow.

Going to the New Hampshire prep school was something Kacie had begged to do ever since the girls attended New England summer programs when they were 14 and 12. While the Exeter application was pending, I'd gaze out over our hillside of California live oaks toward the bare branches of the buckeye trees, and I'd feel absurdly rejected because she wanted to leave home, putting the whole expanse of the country between us. My mind would replay her animated descriptions of elliptical seminar tables with just a dozen students in a class and the thrill of living in a dorm where her father had lived at her age. She had no concern over the three time zones of separation; she was looking forward to fall foliage and snow. Even though I realized that Exeter offered welcome academic challenges and an opportunity for her to grow more independent—and it seemed good that she felt ready for all that—I didn't feel finished raising her. It was too soon. I'd sit in the studio and stitch, think, and pray.

After the acceptance letter arrived, Toby told me, "Since you're having such a hard time letting her go, maybe you need to take her." So I helped her pack and traveled east with her. I dropped her off for transfer student orientation on September 10, 2001. The next morning alone in my hotel room, I watched the World Trade Center attacks live as I was packing to leave. I was gripped with a fear of World War III, this one on American soil. How could I face leaving my firstborn on the East Coast and being away from my husband and *baby* on the West Coast? My flight home out of Boston's Logan Airport was grounded, and even if it hadn't been, I wasn't about to board an aircraft.

Three days later I shared a rental car from Exeter to Chicago with three other new students' moms, all of us in shock and holding each other up as we left our daughters in New Hampshire. I then took Amtrak from Chicago to California, talking endlessly with strangers who seemed like friends in the aftermath of the horror that drew us all close. Both nights I curled up under a thin sweater on the floor between seats, but sleeping was difficult. By day I worked on lesson plans for the class I'd soon be teaching on the spirituality of quilting, and I held my emotions in check until I could be home with Toby and Brenna.

Back home as the weeks passed, I busied myself with quilting to keep myself from feeling devastated about Kacie being 3,000 miles from home, only ten miles from the Seabrook Nuclear Power Plant (which I was afraid might be a terrorist target), and about my being so out of her life. My calls either reached her voicemail or found her too busy for me. "Hey, Mom, good to hear your voice, but I have thirty pages to read tonight. Sorry, can't talk." "Whoa, Mom, I'm on my way to lacrosse, so can you call another time?" Lonely for her, I sent e-mails averaging a half a page a day, and got no more than twenty-five words a week in response. Our Parents' Weekend visit ended badly on a rainy sidewalk as we headed toward the small dorm room she wanted to keep us out of because she needed her space. We'd enjoyed seeing the art department where Kacie spent some of her favorite hours and the dining halls where she ate with her new friends, but we'd offered unsolicited advice and asked nosy questions. She spit out the last word like venom when she asked, "Why do you guys always have to act so parental?"

A Teen Pregnancy Challenged Each Family Member Differently

A couple of years later while Kacie was a spring semester college freshman, Brenna, then 16, got pregnant and chose to keep her baby. We took one day at a time through the pregnancy. My faith sustained me, and God constantly sent us signs and messengers of encouragement. Kacie was home that summer but returned to college in August. A few days later, seven weeks before her due date, Brenna's water broke, and she was admitted to the hospital. Twice a day I visited, playing Scrabble on Brenna's bed, doing appliqué, quizzing the doctors about how to hold off labor, and later asking when it might be safe to induce. Every day Brenna—and some days Toby and I—called Kacie to keep her posted.

Kacie and Brenna together the summer that Brenna was pregnant. Photo by Toby Smith

Three weeks before the due date, an ultrasound finally signaled that the baby's lungs were mature enough to breathe on their own. We had twenty-four hours' notice that induction would start, and no assurances as to when the baby would be born. Kacie was taking five demanding classes. We didn't want her to have a hard time catching up. Toby called the frequent flyer desk to book a flight for her. On Tuesday night, nurses moved Brenna to the labor and delivery ward and hung the drip to start labor. It was Thursday by the time Brenna gave birth to her son, Elliott. Friday morning Kacie flew home to meet him over a long weekend.

I'd anticipated that vacations would bring our family back together, but Kacie worked two summers at a Farm & Wildness Camp in Vermont and spent part of another summer traveling in Europe following a semester in Florence. She took one year off school and supported herself. When she did come home, she often had a boyfriend from the East Coast with her. We imposed limits on car borrowing, music volume, obscene language, and at-home intimacies. We really wanted her more to ourselves, and we unrealistically yearned for our household to have its previous look and feel. Clinging to the old ideal of our obedient little angels, we only managed to have Kacie and her young boyfriend leave the house in a huff.

A Well-Intentioned List Triggered Family Armageddon

That had been the state of things until seven months before the olive branch call when, on another long flight home, Toby and I talked about how our girls were growing up. We lamented how unfinished we felt with our job as parents. I reached under the seat in front of me, pulled out a pad, and we made a list so that we'd be sure to work into coming conversations or activities what we felt we had so little time left to teach. We each jotted down ideas. Practical skills like cooking. Financial skills like putting a budget on paper and simple investing. How to tweak a résumé, network, find meaningful jobs. We edited the list and grouped our goals into categories. We made sure that each item was applicable to both daughters, neither singled out for a lesson that wouldn't benefit both. The finished yellow-lined paper was a mess of scribbles and cross-outs, so the next day I typed and printed it so that Toby and I would have legible copies.

However, I made a big mistake. I left it on my desk.

Kacie and Brenna were both home. It was a Sunday after church, and we were all in my quilting studio discussing what to do after workouts at the gym. Kacie spied the list and asked to see it. We told her no, but she insisted. We relented. Both read it. Brenna found it interesting enough to ask when the cooking lessons would start. Kacie's face reddened as she caught fire.

"You're treating me like a child," she told us vehemently. "I've been perfectly fine living on my own for the past five years, thank you. How dare you ignore my independence and not even ask me what I need? Other people build me up, but you guys are always trying to change me. I'm not that bad, you know—that incompetent, that much of a fixer-upper." According to her, we didn't even come close to understanding or respecting her. If she wanted a job, she could get one, and it didn't have to be a career position yet. She could still opt for fun at 20, and there was nothing wrong with that. "I am not you. My values are very different from yours." She ended her rant by hurling words at me that sent my knight lunging toward her in defense of his bride.

In a rare display of temper, Toby chased her out of the kitchen, out of the house, and down the driveway but then stopped (or was stopped by guardian angels) and let her go. An hour later Kacie came back to the house, and they exchanged short apologies. I was speechless, asking myself how horrible a mother I'd been and at the same time half-waiting for an apology to me too. None came. Nor did I offer one. As the week progressed, she disregarded our every request and repeatedly stayed out late with Toby's car, waking us at three in the morning on work nights. Finally the three of us sat down for a talk. Still stunned by the Sunday argument, I sat mute as Toby invited Kacie to suggest how we could live together and get along. Kacie said, "I'd rather just find another place to live," and Toby answered, "Fine. Please return my car keys now."

Two days later I drove her to the train. As we drove past beautiful cherry trees in full blossom, she said she hoped she wouldn't have to come under our roof again for the next ten years. All the radiance of spring slipped from my spirit. With a sinking feeling in my gut, I watched her hoist her bags and guitar onto her back as she disappeared into the station.

A Dream Foreshadowed Healing and Inspired Hope

Over the next half year while I wondered if and when I'd ever have a decent relationship with Kacie again, I relied more than ever on my monthly dream group. Our meetings were led by a wise, contemplative, Benedictine abbot with more than thirty years of experience with Jungian dream interpretation. At the workshops and in private he helped me analyze my dreams for "lessons from God's night school." The dreams were a compass for my life.

Finally on that pivotal travel day early in December 2006, Toby and I were sitting in the only two empty seats we could find at the gate of a delayed flight when Toby's Blackberry rang. I heard his cheerful, "Hi, Kacie," and then I saw his eyes widen and his eyebrows rise as he continued, "Yes, she's right here. You want to talk to her?"

After I said hello, she faltered. "When I'm in California over winter break, I … uh … wonder if, um, maybe you'd like to collaborate on … um … a fiber arts project?" Her idea was to combine her drawing, painting and embellishing talent with my fabric and quilting experience. "Maybe we could approach it as, like … a way to heal our relationship," she offered uneasily.

I glanced down at the *Strong Women, Soft Hearts* book in my hands. With tears in my eyes, I replied, "Your timing is perfect. I'd like nothing better."

Three days later I awoke with a dream that I knew was about healing with Kacie. I dreamed of sitting on the edge of an operating table that was lifting me several stories to where my clogged arteries would be repaired. I wasn't strapped on or sedated, and I was proceeding to serious heart surgery without a second opinion. I risked falling off the rising table as well as not coming through the surgery. Next thing I knew, I was out of surgery and driving to the dentist.

The abbot, who was also my spiritual director, had taught me that dreams rarely mean what appears at face value, so I didn't worry that mine meant my high cholesterol was heading me for surgery. I needed to couple universal symbols with personal associations. The need for an operation most likely indicated a sick inner attitude that needed repair, so that blood could flow freely again, unhindered by the emotional clog in my heart. The dream showed me that no second opinion was necessary because inner wisdom (the divine physician) would assist in the healing. Waking to the mundane (going from anesthesia to the dentist) told me I would come out of the period of withdrawal, but I'd still need to pay attention to what came out of my mouth.

In the next two weeks, I prepared for Christmas without my usual bah-humbug attitude toward maternal responsibility for the holidays. A part of me had been concerned that our project, though well intentioned, might lead to another explosion. I was grateful that Kacie would be staying at the apartment her sister and nephew had moved into, which was about twenty minutes from our house. But the dream made me hopeful. Knowing that Kacie wanted to reconcile with me and that we were going to do something about it raised my spirits higher than the bright star atop the tallest Christmas tree in town. My innermost self absolutely *knew* that healing was coming. Faith and trust were alive.

Collaboration Began Tentatively, and the Process Worked!

When Kacie walked in the front door and put her arms around me on December 17, my soul shouted a silent alleluia. Two days later Kacie and I began our collaboration. On her laptop she'd collected images in a folder labeled "Mom Project." She suggested I print the ones I liked. We added a few images I'd saved. At her suggestion we decided to take turns selecting elements from the various images to inspire our quilt, a wall hanging.

"Is it okay for me to start by selecting the format of that print of yours?" I asked. "I like your border with its stripes suggesting perspective."

"Sure, that works." In her sketchbook she drew the three-sided border. "I like the three circles in the lower left border and see them each hand-quilted and applied in a 3-D way," she said. "I'd like one to show a bowl of spaghetti."

Our Italian heritage, our favorite food, or her time in Italy? I wondered. She'd suggested that she and I not relive our past while we were working on the project. It'd be enough, she said, to let the collaboration and the art do the healing without having to analyze and rehash. *Wise choice. Easier too.* And my dream had already warned me to be careful about what came out of my mouth.

When it was my turn, I said, "I'd quilt a labyrinth in one," because I'm interested in walking the spiritual path.

And so it went as we alternated tentative choices of various design elements. After a while Kacie pointed to a row of birds. "I'd like to silk-screen birds in flight, but birds don't remind me of anything," she said.

"Interesting," I said. "Those are seagulls, which have a lifetime of meaning for me. First they symbolize the beach, which I love and miss." Without saying so, I thought, *Maybe Newport Beach, the town of her birth and happy elementary school years?* I continued, "Second, to me flight represents freedom." *That's good*, I thought. *Freedom from the prison of an assaulted relationship.*

We Survived a Test in the Middle of Our Collaboration

By dinnertime we had the quilt designed. Afterward at the kitchen table over chocolate chip cookies with her dad there too, she brought up a two-year-old hurt. "I never told you how angry I am that you guys made a decision to exclude me from a really key family event, being there when Brenna had her baby. Didn't you ever think how you made me lose an opportunity that's never repeatable?"

Toby and I listened and sympathized and then asked, "How could we have gotten you a flight during the school week when the time of birth couldn't be known? Besides, how many days could you miss at Wash U? And we arranged it so you saw Elliott when he was only one day old." We reminded her what a tough time those months had been for all of us, the strain we were all under, making all rational thinking a challenge. After another twenty minutes of listening to Kacie's feelings, Toby and I acknowledged that an explanation couldn't undo the loss. We told her we hoped she could understand. Though problematic and maybe naïve in retrospect, our decision wasn't uncaring, just practical.

In times past a tearful conversation like that, one involving bottled-up hurt and resentment, would lead me to withdraw. I would keep my tongue and my distance, thinking there was nothing I could do to make it better like I had over the fight about the list. I'd tell myself that I'd done what I thought was best at the time and yet had failed my daughter. I would beat myself up over the past and fear saying something to make it worse. She'd withdraw too, perhaps focusing on how she'd opened up a wound only to have salt poured into it.

That evening, however, we went back to the studio instead—to a room in which we weren't verbally rehashing the past. We started pulling fabrics from my stash. We began with the colors we came up with in the afternoon. After we had forty fabrics out, we looked at one rich geometric print, and without a moment's hesitation, we decided to abandon all previous colors and use that as the focal fabric, necessitating a trip to the fabric and art stores in the morning.

Suddenly it was midnight, time for her to go back to her sister's. Instead, she went downstairs, stripped down to her T-shirt, and climbed into her old bed. In our own bed Toby and I held hands and uttered an ardent "Thank you, Lord."

The next day Kacie and I got a silk screen, paints, and fabric—not all quilter's cottons but fabric more suited to mixed fiber arts, including hand dyes, sleazy synthetics, organza, and burlap. Later she prepared the silk screen to print gulls onto the border fabric, while I started on the circles. She showed me how to silk-screen. We both covered the dining room table with newspapers, mixed paint colors, spread out the fabric, and pulled paint across the screen, leaving teal gulls on a rust batik. After a long day side by side we hugged and kissed good night, and she spent the night again.

Back in the studio the following day I expressed my reservation about hand stitching the circles. "I think hand quilting will be too slow. You know, I'm mostly a machine quilter."

Kacie stood her ground. "I see the circles hand quilted. That's the way I envisioned it."

After several attempts I stopped trying to change her mind, marked the labyrinth, and dug in. As my stitches walked the path, I enjoyed watching the labyrinth unfold. It was small enough that I finished it in an afternoon. *A lesson there*, I told myself. *Be more open to her ideas instead of trying to control all the decisions.*

I expected to quilt the feather she'd chosen for another circle, letting her do the bowl of pasta, which didn't appeal to me. But no, I had to mark the feather and let her do the hand quilting. Another letting go.

Earlier in the design phase on one of her turns, Kacie had decided to use the inspiration of Brian Andreas's *StoryPeople* for the largest section of the quilt. His were paintings or sculptures made of brightly colored shapes, and most carried signs with clever wording on them. We chose to make people of fabric shapes and decided, after brainstorming, to depict them making pasta, an activity we enjoy as a family. We chose yellow rickrack to represent a long strip of cranked out pasta.

A Clash of Approaches Is Overcome

After we got the basic parts of the quilt executed, we came to some real differences in approach. I stood back and talked about line, balance, unity, moving the eye around the piece, negative space, and the lack of an X in the composition. Kacie said, "I've noticed that you seem to analyze every step of the way. I like to design intuitively."

"I guess you think of yourself as a natural artist, and you are," I replied. "I think of myself as a quilter who's taken classes on the principles of design."

"I just go with what I like," she continued.

Still, the lack of a unifying theme was really bothering me. *Hmmm, a metaphor for the recent stage of our relationship?* What did the silk-screened seagulls, the pasta-making people, and the hand-quilted labyrinth, feather, and bowl of pasta have in common? What could give us thematic unity so we'd have something more than just a collection of elements culled from art we liked, more than just a project to work on without a message?

That night I prayed for a theme, awoke with a concept, and journalled until I had a sentence. Kacie and I tweaked it together. Everything represented slow hand work—making pasta the old-fashioned way, quilting the traditional feather, creating the border by making our own seagull drawing, preparing the silk screen, and painting the fabric in several steps. Even walking a labyrinth is slow and deliberate, part of a long, spiritual path. A mutual goal is the freedom to soar like gulls, to rise above our conflicts.

It all takes time. And so we ended up deciding to change the third circle from a bowl of spaghetti to a clock.

Kacie allowed me to add dots to help move the eye around. My idea was to have them be portions of a circle, representing chunks of time, but Kacie was right. They looked like Pac-Men. We printed the theme sentence on fabric, mounted it on burlap, and appliquéd it to fill some of the negative space on the silky soft background, coarse on top of delicate, frayed on the edges.

I got over Kacie's inclination toward marking and hand quilting. She got over my inclination toward frequent design evaluations. We benefited from the scheduling of our time, accountability to show up for the work, and the intentionality of working together to improve our relationship. We let the piece evolve. We gained perspective—like the quilting lines chosen on day one of the design process. We even agreed on which music to listen to as we worked—her indie rock, my samba. And we

Chris and Kacie as the top neared completion

chatted, consciously careful about what came out of our mouths.

Kacie knew about my dream. On the fourth day she returned from a routine teeth cleaning and said, "Guess what? The dentist just told me I have to get all my wisdom teeth out before I go back to St. Louis, so that means I have to do it this week." Two days later as I waited at the oral surgeon's office for her to come out of anesthesia and for me to drive her home, I was amused that my dream was doubly prophetic.

Later I checked my dream dictionary and discovered Jung's belief that (to a woman) pulling teeth could symbolize giving birth. That was fascinating because this project gave birth to an art quilt and a new beginning.

In the end Kacie got on the flight back to college after our warmest, longest, most loving embrace in years.

The sentence in the green box on the quilt expresses our broadened view. "Like making pasta and art, quilting by hand, and walking a spiritual path, relationships need time and dedication if they are to reach new heights."

With a most grateful heart, I am blessed to be able to report now (in 2014) that Kacie and I have been close ever since!

Copyright 2007 by Chris Boersma Smith and Kacie Erin Smith, *Like Making Pasta: A Mother-Daughter Healing Quilt* (52" x 49"). Juried exhibit: *Pennsylvania National Quilt Extravaganza 2007* and solo exhibit by invitation, "Story Quilts by Chris Boersma Smith," *The Sea Ranch Association Art in the Office* series, The Sea Ranch, CA, 2011–2013

--- STEPS ALONG A SPIRITUAL QUILTMAKING PATH ---

CONSIDER WHETHER THERE'S SOMEONE WITH WHOM YOU MIGHT WORK ON A FIBER ARTS PROJECT AS AN INTENTIONAL COLLABORATION TO HEAL YOUR RELATIONSHIP.

If so, ask and journal how you can prepare your heart ahead of time? Also ask Spirit or your inner wisdom whether— and if so how—you might implement or tweak this process.

PROCESS (evaluate each step of the process ahead of time):

- Propose and agree to collaborate with a shared intent of drawing closer through the process, allowing the process to be more important than the product.
- Set the time and place for your collaboration, protecting the commitment from outside interference.
- Individually set your intention or pray for healing and for each of you to be blessed with the qualities that will enhance the process.
- Feelings might be journalled, but feeling words are probably best left out of the collaborative part of the project.
- Each person begins collecting images or ideas in a project file. Ideas might include doodles or words.
- The first step together is to spread out all the images on a design wall or flat surface. Explain briefly what attracted you to the images you bring to the project.
- A fair and operative framework is to alternate making decisions.
- In most cases, it would be best to keep focused on the project and not to delve into conversation about potentially volatile topics while you are working.
- Stay in the present moment.
- Use paper and colored pens to sketch out a design, at least as you begin. Take turns selecting one element of design, with one person deciding how to proceed with it. These elements may include: theme, size, format, style, line, shape, color, repetition, aspects of harmony and unity, techniques for various parts, embellishments, surface designs, borders or edge finishes, etc. The person exercising a choice may say, "I'm thinking of choosing X because—" The idea is to remain open to the other's input in a collaborative spirit. And when it comes to making a choice, the one whose turn it is gets to make the final choice, with or without taking the other person's input into account. This way each gets to be heard and to control half the decisions. (Feel free to make this less formal if you both work more spontaneously.)
- Once the basic design is sketched out, set it aside and take a break—at least as long as a meal, maybe overnight or longer.
- Play with fabrics. Pull out a variety and keep making combinations by adding and subtracting from the pile until you both feel good about what might be used for the various parts of your design.
- If there are overnight breaks, ask for dreams or inspiration to come to you, put paper and pen at your bedside, expect to wake up and record what comes to you.
- By this point, discussion of how to decide who does what should be rather smooth, as you'll be working simultaneously. Division of responsibilities could be on the basis of skill sets, areas of the studio, or techniques (i.e., one fusing and another machine sewing, one painting and the other piecing, each doing parts she designed, etc.).
- At least every few hours, take time to stand back and look at the work. Be open to learn from each other. Although the process is more important than the result, trying to allow a good product to

emerge is still worthwhile. This is a time for constructive critique, but comments need to be shared with sensitivity and the relationship goals in mind.
- Determine how or if you will share custody or to whom the quilt will be donated or gifted. Naming should be a fun final step too. Keeping a quilt for six months and then trading is a good option if you can't decide. Flip a coin to see who has first dibs. Plan to take good photos so you can each have pictures even when you don't have the piece.
- Decide on basic quilting design and density, and choose threads visually by laying lots of them on the top and perhaps using color photocopies of a digital picture of the top to draw out various proposals.
- Split up responsibilities and do the quilting and finishing as time permits—together or apart.
- As you approach the end of the project, conversations about what the process achieved may be rewarding.
- Photograph the finished work.
- As collaborators, you might even enter the finished piece into a show. Sharing the finished product and the story just may inspire others to allow Spirit and Creativity to heal other strained relationships, and you'll have helped to heal the world two hearts at a time!

REMEMBER:
- Pray or meditate first, before you dive into this process. Don't undertake this without seeking spiritual guidance before and during the process.
- Time is a healer in this process. Don't rush it.
- Making the parts and deciding who makes what will take cooperation.
- Especially if you're the more experienced quiltmaker or artist, remember the goal is healing; the product is only secondary.
- Fabric selection or creation (dyeing or painting it) can be especially fun, lightening up the atmosphere and allowing for a more joint decision-making process.
- Remember, no two people will have matching approaches, assessments, or critiques, and there's always something to learn from another person's input.
- Custody battles are no fun, so plan ahead to avoid them.
- Honesty with sensitivity is key. Remember that actions speak louder than words.

ALTERNATIVES FOR HEALING RELATIONSHIPS: Heart work can also heal relationships, even without the participation of the other person. By "heart work" I mean an intentional and usually guided approach to ridding one's heart of unresolved or residual anger, hurt, and pain by completing forgiveness of situations involving other persons, ourselves, and/or God. Although you may have already done some forgiveness work, the Clean Sweep heart work I've experienced and been trained to do (after this project with Kacie) walks you through a deep and very effective multi-step process. If I'd known about this sooner and/or if I'd offered the olive branch myself much sooner, my relationship woes might not have needed this project, or the collaboration might have brought about our reconciliation sooner. See the final chapter or e-mail me for more on this process.

SHARE: Of all the chapters' suggested reflections and activities, this is the one closest to my heart, so I'd love to hear if you've given this a try or found other ways to use quiltmaking or textile art for healing relationships. Please feel free to email chris@reapasyousew.com or to submit a guest blog post on the subject.

Striped Dress: Annie's Discoveries about Art and Beauty

On rare occasions you meet someone who will affect the rest of your life. You instantly feel it, even if in the beginning the person presents a conundrum.

Calling me moments after I hit SEND to broadcast my e-mail seeking interviews with non-Christian women who feel a spirituality-quilting connection, Annie Beckett jumped right into the topic. She described quilting as "an instant portal" for her. Smiling, I visualized John Malkovich sliding down into some strange reality. But I knew what she meant. Fabric, composition, and colors, she said, give her a God or bliss experience, moments when all locations dissolve into one, when everything connects.

In our twenty-minute phone chat we found we had much in common. Her daughter Ali was just graduating from the same college my daughter Brenna was entering. At the height of our careers as intense overachievers, we'd both burned out from pushing ourselves hard. When she gave me directions to her home, I knew that it was the mysterious house I'd been scrutinizing on my sunset walks since I began coming to The Sea Ranch a few months earlier. It had a glass block wall adjacent to my usual path, a sharply pointed room closest to the bluff, and a detached cottage. After sundown I'd glimpse through the acute angle to the lit kitchen beyond, noticing the shadowy movement of people whom I sensed loved to cook. Of more than two thousand properties on The Sea Ranch, it was the one I knew best after my own and my closest friend's. Annie and I were both drawn to the North Coast to slow down, to honor a Sabbath period of our lives. And we each spoke of having explored various spiritualities.

When we set up our appointment to discuss the connection between her spirituality and her quilting, the quilt she told me about on the phone was an art quilt she made for a curated show. Indeed, while the quilt was still just a conceptual proposal, it was juried into an exhibition featuring nine regional quilt artists and twelve nationally known quilters, including Michael James, Libby Lehman, and Jane Sassaman.

Annie's house in The Sea Ranch, CA

Officially, she told me, the 2006 Gualala Arts Center show was called *4 x 4 x 12 by 3 x 3 x 9*, and it was an exhibition of art quilts from the Penny Nii Collection and Mendocino and Sonoma County artists. Annie's entry was called *Striped Dress*, and I was eager to see the work of this local art quilter who'd been so honored to have her innovative work exhibited with the work of a dozen professional textile artists.

Since our connecting seemed like kismet, it was only natural for the slight, wispy-white, curly-haired, smiling Annie and me to hug when we first met. With a glance into the sharply angled living room from the open kitchen with its Wolfe range, we walked, tea in hand, to her detached quilting cottage to begin our talk. As soon as I walked into this retired Hollywood screenwriter's quilt cottage, my eyes did a double take. They'd just landed on her design wall. A simple patchwork quilt in progress showed that Annie was playing with old-fashioned, large brown, soft pink, and powder blue florals. I saw a traditional quilt of all muted nautical fabrics draped over her white linen loveseat. She told me she'd recently completed it for her daughter Ali's longtime boyfriend, every fabric chosen to honor his interest in seamanship.

One of Annie's traditional quilts, a special gift for Ali and Luc

Baffled at the quilt cottage full of traditional quilts, finished and in process, I silently sipped my herbal tea and reached for a piece of the gluten-free, dairy-free, sugar-free coffee cake she set on coffee table before us. We even followed the same quirky diet. We talked of spirituality before we spoke of *Striped Dress*, which was nowhere in sight.

On the phone Annie had described her spirituality as *eclectic*, which I felt I understood. Eclectic is how I used to describe my décor—an antique pine quilt cabinet, a glass-topped panther coffee table, Restoration Hardware slipcovered chairs, red painted Chinese boxes, and a curvy walnut Victorian settee upholstered in red and cream striped satin—a little of this and a little of that. Each piece was interesting and useful. Somehow they all worked together, and the mix was enriched and made more fascinating than if everything came as a matched set. Sitting in her cottage, Annie explained that she was raised in a casually Protestant home, later studied in various traditions, including Ayurveda, Christian mysticism, Buddhism, and Sufism, and she was now learning Hebrew and converting to Judaism. She observes Shabbat and enjoys a Reconstructionist community led by a female rabbi who is, incidentally, also a quilter.

The interview was the first one for my first book, so Annie's career as a Writer's Guild Award-winning screenwriter awed me. I'd googled her and learned she'd written *First Do No Harm*, starring Meryl Streep (who won an Oscar for the film), based on a true story of an effective but discredited dietary treatment for epilepsy. Annie explained the twofold success of that film. It allowed her to retire, capping off her career, and it improved lives based on what viewers learned from the film. Her talent at storytelling captivated me as she relayed how her quilting and her *Striped Dress* art quilt came to be.

Stressed Screenwriter Finds Respite in Fondling Fabrics and Quilting

One day when she was a screenwriter, Annie had stumbled into a quilt store. Afterward, on particularly hectic days she'd go there to absorb and touch fabrics and to soothe herself. She bought what pleased her, enrolled in a piecing class, but dropped it. Her work put her under stressful deadlines. During the writing she would live the characters' feelings as if they were her own. She used quilting while she was gestating her writing. The visual-tactile-technical nature of quiltmaking engaged her left and right brain. The attention to detail forced her to be present and attentive to something outside her screenwriting. Her racing mind slowed down while she was quilting. Thus restored temporarily, she'd go back to her work.

Typically in the final hours of a screenwriting project, she'd sense that the script was okay. But once it was turned in, she'd feel exhausted, spent, and emotionally flat. Later during filming she consulted. She reworked dialogue the actors felt their characters wouldn't say just that way, and that was the part of her screenwriting role she liked best. After she enjoyed the filming of *First Do No Harm*, she flew from the movie set to her first quilting class—five days at Asilomar with Ruth McDowell no less. She'd just had the best experience of her writing career, and she knew the movie would do well. She called her agent and announced that now she was going to be a quilter rather than a screenwriter!

She packed up and went from commuting between LA and The Sea Ranch to living on the Sonoma Coast full-time. Unfortunately she also faced years of adrenal exhaustion and severe environmental sensitivities. Slowed down and feeling ill much of the time, balancing rest on one end of the scale and homeschooling Ali on the other, she began to quilt more often and more spontaneously. No rules. No deadlines. No pressure. This slow and open (and sensate rather than cerebral) approach metaphorically coincided with the process of finding out in this new life stage just what she needed to do as well as what or who she needed to be.

Annie began nurturing her truer self and a new life for her family—a down-to-earth life, a life in which mother and daughter were together almost constantly. She had endured the earlier but never-ending loss of her 13-year-old son, Gregg, who'd died in an accident before Annie and her husband adopted Ali. She endured challenging health as well as helping Ali address her adoptive pain. Along the way she quilted, managed to exhibit and sell a few quilts, and taught a color class for the local guild.

Annie particularly enjoyed a dozen annual retreats with an art study group that would share and formally critique one another's work. I related very much when she described the lure of this dedicated, focused, female community. We agreed that these gatherings were spiritual experiences that filled a gap in our culture, a part of us that missed the ancient tribe, a yearning for richness, common language, experience, mutual support, and commitment to one another. *The Red Tent* came immediately to my mind, and how appropriately, I thought, as Annie was soon to celebrate her conversion to Judaism.

An Iconic Outfit Triggered a Formidable Quiltmaking Experience

We switched to the topic of family. Hearing about Annie's own childhood and then the one she created for her daughter struck me like a plunge from any icy pool into a hot tub. "Growing up, my family moved thirteen times in twelve years. My father said expressing affection was too close to sentiment, a cheap thing, and so he didn't show it or even say, 'I love you.' Throughout my childhood, he'd tell me, 'You're on your own, kid.' In a wild contrast," as Annie put it, "my love for Ali oozes from my veins. Here in this idyllic community, we've lived in the same house for decades." Annie's hands went to her heart and then opened out. She looked at me, and her voice got softer. "In homeschooling her, I honored Ali's interests, covering the basics but gearing it to specifically engage her interests, like marine biology or whatever was captivating her at any given period." Annie shook her head and pursed her lips. "And yet," she went on, "Ali had ferocious emotions, howling to get out over the years, all bursting from the loss and displacement of knowing she was adopted."

When Ali went away to college, their parting was more of a peeling apart than most mother-daughter duos. One fall day just after she left, Annie was rummaging through and cleaning a high closet shelf like a mother often does when the last child moves out. She came across a little blue striped dress and the brown sandals with flower perforations and tiny buckles that had been Ali's when she was three. Annie remembered saving the little dress, moving it from LA to the seacoast, where it had laid on that closet shelf ever since. The dress and shoes were iconic of a blissful childhood, she thought, but they were misleading. The irony hit Annie hard.

About that time (2005) the Gualala Arts Center (in the Mendocino County town just north of The Sea Ranch) announced that it would host an exhibition of the Penny Nii collection. Excited that the collection of twelve 48" x 48" contemporary art quilts by nationally and internationally known artists would be publicly exhibited for the first time at its gallery, the exhibition's curators wanted to expand the show with nine 36" x 36" art quilts from the local community. They set forth an elaborate application process. Proposals had to be submitted by a late-September deadline. Besides the entry form, artists were asked to submit a three-page write-up of the proposed work, a full-page sketch or photograph of a layout on a design wall, a written description of the design, planned techniques for execution, ideas for color and embellishment, a description of the maker's intent or vision, and optional photographs of previous work.

Writing proposals was old hat for Annie. The timing coincided with her finding the blue striped dress, and she went for it. However, the nerve-wracking application process might have been a portent.

She was advised of her proposal's acceptance on October 10, 2005. The quilt was to be delivered by January 31, 2006. Annie's assumption was that the process of creatively expressing a fraught concept or experience—in this case, Annie's response to Ali's anguish—would somehow exorcise it, advance her insight about it, or at least relieve some of Annie's rather extensive residual distress around her memory of her daughter's adoptive pain and anxiety.

Ali had been a two-pound, six-ounce preemie, adopted in an open adoption and brought home when she was just four pounds. She had a relationship with her birth mother and birth aunt. She experienced ongoing separation anxiety, hypervigilance, and insecurity that prevented her from napping or going to sleep alone. She was reserved and often flinched, yet in that striped dress she looked like an innocent, carefree girl with no troubles or worries. Annie had one surviving older son, her husband had three sons, and Ali was their youngest. Annie knew that Ali always felt different, not in a good way.

Trying to dredge up and express all this from deep within through a prescribed format with a preapproved plan on paper to meet a deadline, letting an important subject matter be hung out in a public venue—well, let's just say Annie was not her calmest and best self. The work was in no way nurturing, focused, or gently proceeding as she found her creative way. Instead, four in the morning would find Annie and her racing mind in her quilt cottage, affixing ribbons, trying to get them to trail just right. It was the dark of winter. Three hours later it was still dark—outside and inside. At one point Annie panicked that the sun had gone out. Had she lost her mind?

Showing the finished quilt was even worse for Annie than making it. Annie had shown some of her quilts in public before, but this higher-profile show put Annie in a time machine that took her back to her screenwriting days. The opening of the show reminded her of reading the critics' reviews the mornings after first airings when the *Hollywood Reporter* and *Variety* would come out, one with a review she'd want to frame for posterity and the other saying the same piece should've been trashed. "I am not my script," she'd have to tell herself then. In both instances, she felt like a deer in the headlights of publicity.

Detail shows one of two faces, representing Ali's two mothers

Though Annie still loves the art of quilting, she has not made another art quilt since *Striped Dress*.

While creatively expressing strong emotional issues in a quilt may bring catharsis for some, for Annie the *Striped Dress* experience brought her a double-whammy of self-discovery. First the process took Annie back to her earlier work life of stress, deadlines, striving to communicate deeply with a public audience, and trying not to identify personally with critics' comments. Her response reinforced her resolve to not overcommit herself as well as to live more in the present and in the presence of the sacred. Secondly the subject matter reopened all the old tensions and turmoil of the past. She relived it without being delivered of it.

Expressing Creativity This Way Revealed the Importance of Living in the Present

It's important to discern what Spirit is revealing to you individually. Annie learned from her *Striped Dress* experience that, at least for her, undertaking to express the beautiful, the joyful, the abundant, the grateful, the pleasurable, the healed, and the whole—that is her way to Spirit.

"And maybe," Annie wrote to me after three meetings, "though we may not imagine how or why, it is the deepest way of remediating the world. The

Copyright 2006 by Ann Beckett *Striped Dress* (36" x 36")

mystical writings of most religious traditions say something about multiple levels of reality, the power of contemplative imagination, as well as the more contemporary focus on mending the brokenness of the world. Before reflecting on what to say about Ali's dress quilt, I never had a feel for what *tikkun* in Hebrew meant."

She went on to explain, "*Tikkun*, out of one, out of the whole undifferentiated consciousness, which was like a perfect vessel, a clay pot, the world was splintered into a million pieces (our experience of separateness), and our task is to mend it and make it whole again." Looking back, Annie acknowledged newfound awareness of the task of putting together what had been broken apart and percolating deep within her for some time. And she was surprised to realize how much it had to do with the changes she was pursuing in her life at the time, not out of a sense of obligation or task-orientation but rather because she felt the desire and an inner tug to do so.

The riddle of the chintz pinwheel quilt on Annie's design wall the day we met was solved. When she described the old-fashioned quilt at that first encounter, her voice was as soft as the chosen fabrics. She spoke of creating quilts in an ecstatic state of bliss, gratitude, and joy. She told me she'd sometimes be sewing and then catch her breath, gasping or crying tears of amazement at the incomprehensible thing it is to be alive, to witness amusing peculiarities, to feel present to the moment. Pointing to white and blue fabrics on her design wall, she said they reminded her of old pinafores and robin's eggs. Then she free-associated to birds' nests and egg hunts as a child. The dusty pink landed her in a summer garden of English roses with her grandmother, who wore old dresses of soft florals and smelled of rose powder that she applied with a puff when she emerged steamy from her bath. Annie then described the wallpaper design over the bathroom cupboard, all told from the viewpoint of a child in awe of her discoveries. This is what she meant with her talk of quilting as an instant portal for her from the physical world to the sacred. It's why she now only makes quilts she loves because they are beautiful to her, even if others might consider them *inane* in their lack of innovation.

Annie contrasts today's prevalent culture with this state of exquisite presence, the holistic integration of beauty that is not self-indulgent, pleasure without regard for the puritanical, indeed amusement at finding spirit and joy inseparable. More concretely we spoke of what she found in Judaism, which has fascinated her since high school when her closest friends were Jewish.

Annie now makes Shabbat with only one requirement, that everything be beautiful—the candles, the setting, the food, the pleasures, and the intimacy. She applies the same requirement of subjective beauty to her quilting.

In 2008, Annie's son Eric was married in a traditional Jewish wedding. The ceremony was so intimate (despite its guest list of three hundred) and so moving that Annie's mother, who had not been interested in talking to Annie's about Annie's affinity for Judaism, took her aside after the wedding and commented, "You must have been Jewish in a former life. I wish I could go back and get married again like this. I get you now."

She told me about the high holy days with her congregation. She began with the goals—a memorial, approaching the gates of renewal, a journey from the faulty self in the world through a month of self-examination to states of imperfection … yet without striving for unattainable perfection, remembering that we are here for a short time, addressing fear and pain, and culminating in a triumphal ram's horn that shreds human feeling and marks the end of these Days of Awe.

I was intrigued at how Annie observed the different states of being at a daylong service as a metaphor for the levels or depths of distraction versus attention with which people approach life. In the beginning she observed (maybe even congratulated herself) that she was here and doing this. After a time she wondered when it would end. She found herself bored and fidgeted for a while. She wanted to get out, to go get coffee, which would have been perfectly fine with the congregation, but she also didn't want to miss any part of the service. Finally she was purely present—in that room with the people standing with arms encircling one another, chanting, dusk settling in—and at the end, there was just the light of one candle. The effect was unifying oneness.

Annie and I discussed Eckhart Tolle's interpretation of Jesus' saying, "I am the way."

"Jesus was so Jewish and so mystical," she says. "I Am. Here and now. Here and now is the way. Quilting simply beautiful quilts is a part of the here and now for me. It is mystical."

Getting to know Annie, her story, and her energy and connecting with each other on so many levels, I couldn't stop thinking of the parallels between Annie's journey and my own, including the frenzy of the lawyer and the screenwriter with adrenaline-fueled productivity, spiritual seeking, quilting providing therapeutic relief and a spiritual path, loving our daughters through traumas that wrenched their mother's guts, and retreating to the tranquility of the seacoast. But I saw myself having completed the inward path like I would in a labyrinth, entering with some confusion and an intent to learn what needs to be learned and then hanging out in the center and, since meeting Annie, joining her on the path out, having gained important insight, enjoying the release that comes after discovering what one needs to discover.

I admire the part of Annie that loves the present and the part of her that says, "I can only do so much, and I choose to do what I truly want to do." And it's all good because what the spiritually aware person wants to do is pure and comes from the sacred true self within. I found that I wanted to tell Annie's story about the *Striped Dress* quilt and what went into it, but more importantly I cared about how afterward she had chosen to make quilts that delighted, ones that were still meaningful but without the striving that could take the joy out. I see how she focuses more on being and on feeling than on doing to attain certain results. In the end I'm more affected by what I see in Annie and how she approaches the process even when the product isn't some art quilt juried into a big deal show.

* * *

Quiltmaking and Quilters Provide Comfort

I drafted the preceding story about three years ago, and an epilogue seems a must since it also shows Spirit at work. In the summer of 2012, at 27, Ali married Luc, the young maritimer she'd met when she was volunteering on historic ships at San Francisco's Hyde Street pier. They'd loved each other since they were 14 and 15. After college they bought, lived on, and together restored a fifty-seven-foot wooden schooner docked in the San Francisco Bay. They enjoyed the camaraderie and admiration of their family members and like-hearted people, many of whom were inspired by the authenticity of the lives of two people so connected to each other and so committed to living their dream.

I'd seen Annie getting ready for Ali and Luc's wedding. She sewed an elaborate, vintage, lace-embellished pillow for the ring bearer and showed the pillow and her dress to her art critique group, which I'd been invited to join. The group encourages us to grow in our art, to learn from one another, sometimes to learn from presentations we take turns preparing on a variety of art topics. And since we're deeply connected women, of course we share aspects of our personal lives as well.

Chris Boersma Smith

As Annie approached a milestone birthday, we asked her how she'd most like to celebrate it. She replied that other than the celebration she'd like to have with her husband and family, what she wanted most of all was to have a few days of a quilting retreat. But not one where we'd have to pack and leave town. Just a few days dedicated to sewing with our little group and not letting anything else interrupt us. So we planned just such a retreat around her January birthday when five of us could attend. I offered to host it at my newly finished studio, which was specifically made so that many ladies could all have space to design, cut, sew, and chat in one big room.

On a mid-December evening before Luc was to set to ship out for work, he and Ali, still newlyweds, went out to join friends for a birthday party. Crossing Grand Avenue near Lake Merritt in Oakland, in a crosswalk they were struck by a car traveling too fast. The driver didn't see them. Luke was injured badly but survived. Ali suffered traumatic brain injury and did not.

Two days after Ali's burial Annie and her husband, Jerry, got a call that Jerry's son Dann, who'd been with the family at the trauma center while Ali was on life support, was killed while he was working in Columbia as command pilot of a Chinook helicopter. He was transporting oil rigging when the helicopter broke up in the air and crashed, killing all seven aboard.

Wedding photo of Ali and Luc by Nissa Brehmer

Annie's son Gregg had died as a youngster, riding his bike.

It was just too much.

We assumed the quilting retreat would be canceled or postponed, but no, Annie said she needed it more than ever. She did, and so did we. Annie worked on an appliqué quilt, starting the first of twelve blocks of tall ships from a pattern she'd found and was going to show to Ali over the holidays. Annie is a woman of heart and of words, and she shared both. We talked of Ali and Luc, Annie and Jerry, Gregg and Dann, grief, life, and death. We hugged, and we sewed. We cried, and we ate. Spirit was with us in our deep connecting.

Reap As You Sew

January retreat in Chris's Sea Ranch studio

Grieving and healing are unpredictable and difficult processes, and it's said that grieving the loss of a child is the hardest of all. Annie goes on day by day. She is loved, and she loves. She's forging a new relationship with Ali, one transcending the earthly dimension. And she quilts stitch by stitch, simple quilts and UFOs because she can't yet cope with anything more complex. Every day she does some quilting, even if only a few minutes of hand stitching. Beauty and color are her focus, and her quilting soothes and supports her.

Annie at a design wall during the retreat

--- STEPS ALONG A SPIRITUAL QUILTMAKING PATH ---

CONSIDER WHICH OF YOUR SPECIAL GIFTS AND AFFINITIES ARE AT PLAY IN YOUR QUILTMAKING.
Gifts, styles, and mediums vary. There's room for precision and flexibility, planning and spontaneity, tradition and innovation, working big or small, realism and abstraction as well as folk art, working in a series or a piece at a time, conveying a recognizable theme or not, focusing on process or product . . . and so on all along the spectrum. Maybe you like to intersperse traditional and art quilting, fabric painting and appliqué, depending on your mood, or alternating between them to achieve variety and to have fun with different techniques. Anything goes!

ACT: Do some free (non-judgmental and stream-of-consciousness) writing about your preferences and affinities. Try to include what type of quilt or what part of the process . . .
- makes you lose track of time,
- best engages your imagination,
- promotes daydreaming for you or acts as a portal to reminiscences or discoveries,
- makes you feel challenged and/or courageous,
- frustrates you or makes you feel "not good enough," or conversely, thrills you,
- gives you the most satisfaction or feels most in line with your higher purpose,
- seems like it just takes forever,
- seems most prayerful or spiritually uplifting, and/or
- engages your sense of beauty, wonder or oneness.

LIGHTEN UP:
- Use your favorite fabrics and/or embellishments! Don't let your best just sit there waiting for a perfect project. Be bold and accept that now is the time!
- Discover new threads. Try hand or machine quilting with different weights and different colors for a change. Play with paints or embellishments. Do it just for fun!
- Lower your expectations, at least occasionally. Enjoy the process, adopting a playful and experimental attitude, letting go of perfectionism and of determining whether the resulting quilt is show-worthy. Enjoy the tactile and visual beauty of your materials.

***

IDENTIFY YOUR PERSONAL PALETTE AND HONOR IT. When I moved, I organized the bulk of my fabric stash into the color families in Joen Wolfrum's Ultimate 3-in-1 Color Tool (ISBN: 978-1-60705-235-7, available at http://joenwolfrom.com/color-design-tools/ for $16.95). The tool is a fan of twenty-four cards, each including a pure color plus tints, shades and tones of it (about thirty-four colors per card). I took the tool apart and placed one of the twenty-four cards in each of twenty-four acrylic boxes, and I categorized fabrics accordingly. Chartreuse and orange-yellow required more than one box, which surprised me. I then reviewed my quilts to see how often I used those colors, and I found that I used one or both about half the time; however, they appeared frequently in my favorite and more recent quilts.

This is a big project, so maybe you could just try it with your solids or your fat quarters. If you use the colors of your personal palette (which are likely to shift over time), your work will probably feel more personal, and it also may give you that blissful feeling Annie gets when she's working with the fabrics she now chooses to work with simply because to her they're beautiful.

If She Had Wings: Donna's Imagination

Often reflected in her quilts, Donna Blum's spiritual beliefs are baffling to most people, but her encompassing spirit is widely known. As with Annie and Sue, I found Donna by broadcasting an e-mail to our local guild's membership, seeking interviews with non-Christian spiritual quilters. Donna responded, telling me she was a theosophist and asking how she could help. We exchanged a few e-mails, and although we hadn't yet met, she invited me to come to her Mondays at One Quilt Group.

The first time I went to her house, she whisked me upstairs to introduce me to the forest folk and whimsical creatures flying across her sunny, high-ceilinged studio, where art quilts hung above the cabinets, bookshelves, windows, and design walls. "Most people just don't get these quilts," she said softly. "They like them because they're fantasy, but I don't even try to explain what they mean to me spiritually."

Donna started telling me her story with her father as the leading character. A single parent, he regularly took Donna and her younger brother up the coast, where he was a weekend fish and game warden. Although paid for this weekend work, he considered it a calling to protect the coastal wildlife—sea otters, seals, abalone, and salmon. Combining his love of nature, beauty, and an open mind, he encouraged Donna's imagination.

Grinning and demonstrating with a flower from her courtyard, Donna showed me how he'd pick a double fuchsia and turn it into a ballerina. He used the stem to form the ballerina's outstretched arms. The seed pod became her topknot, the curly dark purple petals, her overskirt, and the pale delicate second layer of petals became the underskirt. The stamen's filaments were her legs, and the anthers were her toe shoes. He'd make her dance in front of young Donna's eyes.

Donna and her fuschia ballerina

Donna Has Experienced a Sampler of World Religions

An Episcopalian with a broader-than-circumscribed view, Donna's father told his children he didn't want them to choose a religion simply because of their parents' tradition. Although the children were baptized and catechized and they made their communions in his church so they'd learn its rituals, teachings, and history, he did so to inform rather than to indoctrinate them. He started exposing them to other churches and religions, suggesting that after they saw that many people accepted different beliefs and lived their lives by different moral compasses, they should make informed decisions for themselves.

As a child, Donna attended a Baptist camp, went to a Lutheran summer school, experienced a Native American sweat lodge, attended services in a Jewish synagogue, and observed Hindu and Muslim practices. With each experience, her father would get to know someone so they'd have an acquaintance to question about the faith. "The concept of Karma was a major moral belief my father taught us. As ye sow, so shall ye reap," said Donna without even knowing the title of this book.

For a while the family attended a Buddhist temple in San Francisco. Her father was attracted to the Shinto belief system of spirits in nature—in plants, animals, and rocks. He was greatly attracted to Japanese landscape design. The family's gardens featured bonsai and flowering Asian shrubs. Donna says the Asian experience must have left a lasting impression because later the family moved to an all-Japanese neighborhood in Sacramento. Donna's brother married a Japanese woman who's a practicing Buddhist, and they raised their children as Buddhists. As for Donna, so many of her quilts have an Asian influence that she wonders if prior lives in the Far East continue to draw her to Asian elements.

Donna's first job after she left home gave her the opportunity to live in a Jewish home. Later she lived and worked in Iran. She had Western-educated Muslim friends who supported openness and outside interest in their faith. On her travels Donna donned the Muslim dress and veil along with sunglasses to hide her blue eyes. Thus covered and using her quickly acquired Farsi, she'd enter the mosques invisibly. She wanted to know from personal experience how Muslims worshipped, how they prayed and related to the mullahs. Hidden behind the veil, she was able to see the intricate mirrored mosaics and watch supplicants seeking comfort before magnificent silver and gold icons.

Donna Became a Theosophist

The man whose photo prominently gazed down on us in his daughter's studio certainly succeeded in encouraging Donna's natural curiosity to explore faith and culture as well as to give full reign to her imagination, her creativity, and her love of nature and the northern California coast. I was fascinated with the pixie-haired woman with a turned-up smile who was standing before me in front of her design wall, her eyes sparkling behind her Jimmy Choo glasses.

I asked Donna whether her sampling of religions ever tempted her to embrace one. "I'm different from most people," she told me, the first of several times she shared that conclusion. "I don't belong to a traditional religion or faith. I'm a theosophist, and we are all-embracing. All godheads and faiths offer ways

Donna Blum at her design wall

for people to be in touch with their spirituality. Most people identify easily with a church or a doctrine that works for them, talks to them, and offers them social and familial comfort and acceptance. I don't. But I have a defined path. I pursue the growth and development of my eternal spirit, and I am content. I—we all—choose our lives daily, whether consciously or not. I believe in self-responsibility for our thoughts as well as our actions. As theosophists, we believe in the Golden Rule and accept that each eternal spirit evolves through many lifetimes. We're here to help, love, and uplift each other, and we build understanding by studying other religions."

Donna told me she discovered theosophy after college when she was teaching art in the San Luis Obispo area. A dear co-worker invited her to come live in Halcyon, a California community begun in 1903 that was centered around its Temple of the People. For five years Donna lived there among many third-generation families of theosophists.

The term *theosophy* comes from the Greek for *divine wisdom*. It's an esoteric philosophy concerning and seeking direct knowledge of presumed mysteries of being and nature, particularly concerning the nature of divinity. Accordingly the theosophist seeks wisdom that offers the individual enlightenment and salvation as well as understanding of the mysteries and origins of the universe and of the bonds that unite the universe, humanity, and the divine. "Everyone there had the same subset of beliefs," Donna told me.

"It must have been hard leaving it," I suggested.

She shook her head. "It was important being around other believers, especially in the beginning. But it's a theosophist tenet that you take the temple with you. It was a chapter in my life."

She doesn't know any other theosophists where she lives now, but she recognizes kindred spirits. She isn't called to proselytize because theosophy is about wonder, openness, tolerance, no accidents, and allowing others to believe what they do, make their choices, and develop according to their own eternal timing in this lifetime or another. "Sometimes I plant seeds though, and occasionally," she said, "I slip and say something about energy or auras or nature that gives me away. And a kindred spirit picks up on it. Like when I told someone, 'I don't think that rock would appreciate your kicking it.' Sometimes I sense a spiritual link with those with nature-based philosophies—and there are many here on the coast—some into moon worship, solstice celebrating, peace and meditation on the beach, or talking to mushrooms. We share the idea that it all fits with our place in the world—listening to its rhythm."

Her Quilts Depict Awe in Ways Children Understand

"The magical creatures in my quilts are meant as reflections of spirit in the world," she explained. "They express my wonder in the world's continual unfolding and endless beauty. Who can question the magic of a phoenix, the soft voice of flowers, the song of the mermaid, or the mythical nature of a sea dragon? Sometimes as people grow older, they lose that magic, the spirituality of the world we live in."

Copyright 2012 by Donna Blum, *Mermaid Magic* (36" x 40), Pacific International Quilt Festival 2012, Santa Clara, CA

Copyright 2010 by Donna Blum, *Sea Dragon*, quilt and two detail views

"How do people respond to your quilts?" I asked. Watching Donna's response was even better than hearing it. She faced me and explained that other religions cherish symbols like the cross or the Star of David, which convey meaning and history. "With theosophy's pervasive view," she said, "trying to pin it down to a symbol would miss the point. No symbol would be sufficiently inclusive for people, nature, the world, consciousness, infinity, everything spiritual." Then she turned and looked with wide-open eyes at her phoenix quilt while she gave me the rest of her answer, her arms moving in circles as big as hula hoops. Her wrists and hands mimicked the bird's wings and indicated its wavy flight path. "I think my dragons, fairies, magical butterflies, flowers that talk, and this phoenix are a translating screen for me, for all that's spiritual for me in the world. And it's okay. It's accepted because the quilts are like childhood fantasy. It's a societally acceptable way of expressing life and nature, wonder and the magic of moonlight, clouds and stars."

For her guild's annual challenge show in 2008, Donna did what she always does. She made a quilt she loved and figured out how to fit it into the challenge. "The theme was 'I found it in the library,'" Donna continued. Initially she had the idea of making a flying dragon, but then she felt inspired to create a phoenix instead. No wonder for someone who believes in reincarnation! The phoenix is a mythical bird with a tail of beautiful jewel-toned plumage. Near the end of its five-hundred-year lifecycle, it builds a nest that it ignites. Both nest and bird burn fiercely and are reduced to ashes, from which a new young phoenix is born to live again, destined to live as long as its old self. The bird may also regenerate when hurt, thus being almost immortal and invincible. Another myth is that the phoenix can heal a person with a tear from its eyes and temporarily render him or her immune to death. In short, the bird symbolizes fire and divinity, an eternal image of healing and rebirth. It symbolizes the endless cycle of nature's renewal as well as the belief in life everlasting.

Buckbeak's Return close-up details

Copyright 2008 by Donna Blum, *Buckbeak's Return* (38" x 48) depicts the magic of eternal renewal as Donna's phoenix is resurrected to fly again in a midnight sky of crystal stars. Pacific Piecemakers' Quilt Guild 2008 Challenge, Members' Choice award.

Before she sketched her design, Donna ruminated, "If I were a phoenix, where would I live? What powers would I possess? What would I see below me as I flew?" She used her active imagination—the one trained with fuchsia ballerinas—and visualized the moon. She envisioned the bird flying across the sky in front of the moon, and she knew she'd add gauzy streams of light showing the bird's slipstream.

"I thought about Buckbeak, a mythical creature from two Harry Potter books. The character was so popular that the author decided to 'bring him back to life' after he'd burned up—precisely what phoenixes do! And I liked him too. So my imaginary phoenix blended with Buckbeak. My bird doesn't resemble Buckbeak on J. K. Rowling's book covers." Indeed, the phoenix in Donna's *Buckbeak's Return* sparkles with Swarovski crystal beads on his wings and tail, and a glittery gossamer trails behind him. I didn't ask about the beading because the shimmery delight that they add seems … well, natural. *Buckbeak's Return*, like many of Donna's quilts, reflects wonder in the world's continual unfolding to each consciousness and the endless magic of living.

Although those with thin skin might not, Donna loves being an anonymous docent at shows where her work is exhibited. "Some people see my fantasy creature quilts, and it's like a lightbulb goes off. They glow as their eyes widen." So did her eyes as she told me this. "If they're with another person, they often turn and link arms with the other or touch them tenderly. They'll often ask me, the docent who they didn't know was the maker, if they can touch the quilt. Some stand back to look at my work, while others practically bury their noses in it. When they do that, I feel as if I'm watching people travel to a magical place that my spirit's creativity made visible." Donna's hands were waving wildly again.

"Others," she told me with sly amusement on her face, "seem to see the word *fantasy* stenciled across the quilt, and they make an abrupt getaway, not the least interested. I mean, when was the last time you found a dragon soaring over your midnight moon?" she asks. "But the children—oh, the children always get it." Donna smiled again.

People who know that she is the quiltmaker often ask Donna where she got the picture. "It's inside," she answers. "That's the world that I see!" They see her so grounded in their everyday world that they assume she copied the various parts from photographs—the bird, the castle, the turrets, the windows. But she didn't. She imagined everything through her artistic gifts—gifts that she believes have been developing over her spirit's earthly lifetimes.

Donna believes that creativity flows through various forms and media. Her business career didn't always provide an opportunity to use that creativity. In retirement and moving to the coast, quilting gave her a much-needed outlet for that pent-up drive to create. She instituted a fiber arts group with a framework for challenging the members to explore light, color, line, form and other elements and principles of design. Donna explained that she often incorporated into larger works what she tried in her monthly 8.5" x 11" studies. The group's mandate was open, so participants could push themselves in their own artistic development in an atmosphere of trust and comfort with authentic expression, opened further by each person's sharing and giving. Gee, sounds a lot like Donna's theosophy, doesn't it?

Spiritual Lessons Are Geared to the Receivers

Although Donna knows she's not treading the standard track, she doesn't feel misunderstood. For example, the local quilt guild's challenge another year was to create a self-portrait. Donna entered *If I Had Wings*, depicting a fairy sitting on a mushroom with a magical snail and a dragon in the tree. She was amazed that perhaps only two of her many friends *got it*. "Clearly not everyone can see your soul. Nor do many comprehend how nature has so much to tell us," she remarked. Donna rejoices when her pieces sell. To her, it means she has touched someone else's soul.

Copyright 2005 by Donna Blum,
If I Had Wings (28" x 42") - detail

She feels she's just in a different space with conscious awareness of who she is and what her path is, and she pursues it contentedly. Some people hold other religious, moral, ethical, and philosophical beliefs that guide their self-development and belief systems, and "they are where they are." That's fine with Donna. She feels no compunction to be understood or to teach others her views. She believes spirituality is the power of perceiving formless spiritual essences in all things. "I find joy and fascination in the variety and endless richness of the human spirit," she purrs as her twenty-two-pound cat, Mikey, jumps onto her lap.

This inscribed stone in Donna's garden reflects the feeling she holds for others. She blesses them on their travels, honoring the peace they hold in their universes as well as the peace she holds in hers.

***

Almost a year after that interview I was working on a seaweed quilt. I was drawn to the subject, I thought, because whenever my dog and I walk the beach—almost daily when I'm at Sea Ranch—my spirits soar. I breathe in the salt air and feel healthy. My eyes linger on all the details—the rocks, the birds, the harbor seals, the waves, the ripples in the sand, the driftwood, and of course, the seaweed. I was composing a somewhat 3-D quilt with layers upon layers, representing long tubular stems of kelp, flowing green sea grasses, dry straw curlicues, and broken pieces of shiny, wet, brown, green, and bleached-out seaweed. I named it as I did because the typical seaweed composition on the beach appears as a tangled mess, a transient still life since each wave rearranges the pile.

These beach walks celebrate the present moment, a welcome change from the frenzy I'd slip into when I dwelled on my complicated day-to-day life—so much to do, my family so scattered, my domicile unsettled as I divided my time between the Bay Area and The Sea Ranch and also traveled with my husband. Years after *Hong Oridney*, questions about our future were again hanging over our heads like spiderwebs (though this time we were calmer). After that Saturday's walk, I met Donna at an art opening, and we went to dinner afterward. "Donna," I said over locally foraged portabellas and greens, "I want to tell you the insight that hit me at the beach today. I finally know why I'm making the seaweed quilt. I am the seaweed! My thoughts and my life are a temporary arrangement of bits and pieces strewn here and there, entangled in some kind of chaos, rearranged by every wave of life, and yet … that mound of seaweed is beautiful, the chaotic way it is, tangled and torn and transient. It doesn't need to be unwound or fixed!"

Donna knew exactly what I meant. "Spiritual lessons from nature," she said. "That's what I love to share. That's what I constantly see, what inspires me."

Nature to her, I thought, *and the Holy Spirit to me. Divine revelation for each of us.*

"I really like you," I blurted out, reaching over and hugging her.

"I love you too," she said, holding the embrace.

Copyright 2010 by Chris Boersma Smith *Seaweed: An Un-Still Life* (32" x 36")

--- STEPS ALONG A SPIRITUAL QUILTMAKING PATH ---

CONSIDER THAT INSPIRATIONS AND GUIDANCE COME TO US THROUGH WONDER AND IMAGINATION.

FIRST SMALL ACTIONS:
- Decide where to keep ideas—visual and verbal—to refer to when you're thinking about a new quilt or just want to let your imagination play. If you don't already have a place for pictures, photos, sketches, or thoughts, designate a physical folder or box, a sketchbook or design journal, an electronic file, and/or a folder in your digital photo files. If you have several of those, put reminders in each place to also check the others. Let's call these places collectively your "Idea Repository."
- Take a walk and look for shapes, colors, or subjects that captivate you. Photograph them and put them in your Idea Repository.
- Observe children without interacting. Note in your Idea Repository what fascinates them.
- Peruse magazines or websites with pictures that catch your fancy. Cut out and/or copy and save your treasures in your Idea Repository, which may include Pinterest or Instagram.

CREATE:
- Focus on one of the ideas from your Idea Repository. Look through your stash and pull out the colors you observed, or the ones your imaginative mood suggests.
- If you prefer traditional patterns, peruse books or the Internet for ones using the shapes you've identified, or blocks named for what you've just observed or imagined.
- To make an art quilt that realistically or abstractly represents a subject from nature, you might start with a 4" x 6" index card, scissors and a glue stick. Cut and paste several small versions inspired by these ideas. If you like one of the small mock-ups, then make it into an actual quilt. Or work in Pamela Allen (*www.pamelart.com*) or Sue Benner (*www.suebenner.com*) style, starting with a small backing, to which you fuse or spray-baste batting, and then make the top by adding fused or spray-basted background and/or pieces to build a pleasing composition. Let yourself play without pressure to create a masterpiece. If you love your play piece, you could quilt it or make a larger version.

***

CONSIDER ENTERING QUILT SHOWS AND PARTICIPATING IN CHALLENGES. Letting a theme or a show motivate you may take you out of a rut or nudge you to try a new approach or express a new idea. You can always decide before the deadline that the timing is too close. The quilt police won't arrest you. Supporting shows, especially local ones, contributes to the world of quilting. There would be no shows if everyone kept their talent at home or only shared it with family and friends.

***

CONSIDER forming or joining a small quilt group or art critique group to enjoy the camaraderie of other quilters and encourage artistic development. There are magazine and online articles with guidelines on how these groups work. Or you can contact me and I'll be happy to share my experiences with groups like that. You could even consider forming an art critique group with people working in other media besides fiber arts. The elements and principles of design and many aspects of the creative process are common to all creatives, and the cross-pollination and objective input from nonquilters can enrich your learning.

Liberty's Timeline Quilt:
A Modern Quilter Pours Her Heart Out

In her thirties, Liberty Worth is unusually young and intentional to be crossing things off her bucket list, but she checked off making a quilt four years ago. She thinks perhaps making one got on the list because her dad was an artist. She'd been raised to believe that being creative was in God's image, and patching together a quilt seemed like a good way to honor that. A fine arts major who'd been making and selling hundreds of handmade skirts online as well as doing collage and assemblage, Liberty was in a neighborhood MOMS club (part of the national Moms Offering Moms Support network). When one woman asked online if anyone wanted to learn to quilt, Liberty jumped at the idea. Three moms began making traditional quilt blocks by scouring for block patterns online. Liberty also watched instructional videos, and the women helped each other figure out techniques. But quilts are like fine chocolates. It's hard to stop at one.

Soon Liberty and some of her quilting friends made the transition from traditional quilts to improvisational modern quilts. A couple of them were among the earliest members to join the LA Modern Quilt Guild, the very first of that trendsetting new movement in the quilt world. Through the guild Liberty made many close friends. And it's a very good thing Liberty had her quilting friends because they supported her when she needed them most.

Modern quilter Liberty Worth

By nature, Liberty is highly energetic, her heart and essence giving off a buzz and colorfulness, yet there's peacefulness about her too. I sensed that from Instagram photos, where she's dressed up as Frida Kahlo, her thoughtful posts, and our conversations. Liberty's done six years of blogging, so with her permission, I'm presenting much of her story in an edited version of her own words.

Liberty's story illustrates three of the spiritual benefits of quilting:
- the already touched-upon relationship-building aspects;
- the opportunity for self-expression, whether

that be therapeutic, artistic, storytelling, or all of the above; and
- the personal spiritual benefits that come from mindfulness or being still, calming one's mind, and receiving spiritual insights and/or healing.

Having grown up surrounded by adopted children, Liberty had a heart not only for adoption but also for providing foster care for little children in the most dire circumstances. She and her husband Jay felt blessed by their faith in God, their love for children, this special calling, and the life circumstances that make it possible for them to be both natural and foster parents. Indeed, they felt that serving as foster parents was their way of serving both God and society.

While their daughter Mimi and son Z were preschoolers, Liberty and Jay began foster-caring for a baby boy called AJ, whom they were trying to adopt. (To protect the children's privacy, all minors are referred to by pseudonyms.) The family was sitting in church one Sunday, and Liberty felt over the moon in love with the idea of how their family was shaping up. Jay was holding AJ as she drew in her sketchbook.

A woman began to proclaim the powerful New Testament verses in Romans 8. "For I am convinced that neither death, nor life, nor angels, nor principalities, nor things present, nor things to come, nor powers, nor height, nor depth, nor any other created thing, will be able to separate us from the love of God, which is in Christ Jesus our Lord" (Romans 8:38–39 NASB).

Liberty knew she needed those words tattooed on her wrist. She wanted to always remember that no matter what the future held, nothing could keep AJ from God's love. Nothing could tear her family's love from one another. And nothing could ever take her away from the love of God.

The next day AJ was suddenly taken from the Worths' home and placed into his sixth temporary foster home in his three-month life. The Worths wouldn't be able to adopt him. Liberty was crushed.

She went ahead with the shorthand version of the Romans message, so her wrist is now tattooed with "Nothing Can Separate Us." Some people think the tattoo sweet and romantic without knowing it actually refers to God's love as well as to Liberty's love for the children she's birthed and those she's attempted to adopt.

Sadly AJ wasn't the only child she lost.

There was Ace a few months later. This time the social worker was set on the Worths adopting him, but every interaction Liberty had with Ace's biological mother told her that she deserved another chance. Liberty didn't believe the bio-mom would hurt her baby. When Ace was moved to another home closer to his bio-mom, Liberty and Jay took a few months off foster care.

When they tried again, they got their precious baby G, who was three weeks old. They were told he was a fast-track adoption, and they desperately wanted to adopt him. Liberty was elated during the short season when they had four kids—their two plus G and a 4-year-old girl who was staying with them. She felt so full of purpose—exhausted in the best way.

In the sad and scary story that follows, Liberty doesn't want to arouse pity or discouragement; rather, hers is a testimony about love and about the role that quiltmaking played in her journey to rebuilding joy. It's about a struggle her family survived. Though it involves death threats and loss, the story is about a marriage committed to the spouses looking at each other eye to eye and never giving up on each other. It's about love being deeper and wider and stronger and more powerful than hate or fear. It's about a God who loves his daughter, even if he let her get broken by pain that came about because darkness as well as light exists in this world.

The short story—because the detailed version

cannot be shared—is that Liberty's family survived fifteen months of threats and harassment. Liberty carried pepper spray with her constantly and became paranoid. She covered baby G's stroller with a screen everywhere she went because she was so afraid of being attacked. Even so, she was a regular mom through this, picking up her kids at preschool and first grade, making dinner, juggling life with three kids, making art, sometimes running her online handmade skirt business, blogging, stitching, and most of all, trying to keep her kids from feeling that life was bordering on insanity. Yet in the end social workers had to bring G down the back stairs because they feared for the foster family's safety.

The Thanksgiving week when the toddler first called her mom, G had to leave. Someone had slipped up and given the biological mother the Worths' address, and she used it in private and public death threats against the family, including Liberty and Jay's two children. Liberty and Jay were the ones who had to make the *Sophie's Choice* and the call to have G moved to a top-secret home—like baby witness protection—to protect G and Mimi and Z.

That's when Liberty realized she had nothing left of herself. She was an open wound, a baby's mother with empty arms who, like the rest of the family, dreams of his return. Mimi and Z, who were then five and seven, were suffering the loss of a brother as well as a lost sense of security.

Within that first month of agony, Liberty's best support came from her quilting friends and some knitters—creative women who didn't try to make sense of it or offer platitudes or try to figure out God's ways. They just sat and stitched with her, providing huge comfort just by being there.

Heart and Hands Created a Textile Time Line and Began Rebuilding Joy

One month after G left, Liberty began to create an abstract timeline story quilt. During the next two months she poured an unfathomable amount of grief, disappointment, anger, devastation, concern for her children, and questions into that quilt. As she puts it, she spent that time "rebuilding joy," her fingers working feverishly to do her heart's work, trying to express her story and relieve her pain in this quilt. Sometimes her grief numbed her so that she was just going through the motions of living, and the quilt gave her hands something to do while Jay watched sports on TV. Sometimes considering the tremendous fallout with her brokenhearted kindergartner and second-grader, working on the quilt helped her focus her brain in one direction. The work calmed her brain enough so that she could stay grounded, even just a bit more than she would have been.

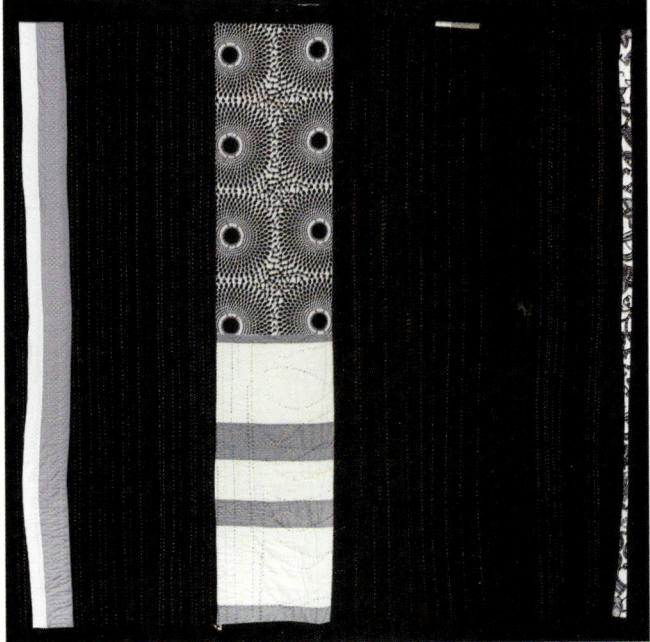

Copyright 2012 by Liberty Worth,
Timeline Quilt, front and back

This quilt was made less than a year after Liberty's quilting had taken a sharp turn in the direction of her other artwork—no rules, no ironing, just liberating improvisation with lots of curves, all coming straight out of her heart. She'd found her voice in a Denyse Schmidt workshop sponsored by the LA Modern Quilt Guild, and she has since employed an improvisational personal style.

This time she improvised with stripes of varying widths and fabrics. With each stripe representing a different period in G's life, Liberty processed her emotions, and her pain became a little less overwhelming as she worked. She says Spirit helped her heal and walk through her heartbreak. She was still and mindful while documenting the family's history with G. She put into the timeline hundreds of hours and thousands of stitches, including hand quilting with perle cotton. The hand quilting alone would probably have taken many of us the amount of time it took Liberty to do the entire project.

Shortly before the Timeline Quilt was finished (on Liberty's 2012 leap-year birthday), Mimi watched her stitch and asked, "Momma, what's the story of that quilt?"

The question itself amazed Liberty because she'd never before made a quilt with a story. She laid the quilt on the ground and began to ask Mimi questions. "Who do you think might be the red? And the gray? And the other parts, what might they be?"

And then she pointed to the area with the curved piecing. It represented the boiling point, when it felt like the family was in a fire. She told Mimi, "This part is the struggle." And Liberty then had to explain to her 7-year-old what the word *struggle* means.

The black fabric with white text, before and after the wide band representing the struggle —Mimi saw that and asked, "Momma, are these the lies and scary things that were said to you?"

The little hands of the two tiny people behind the quilt in this photo belong to Mimi and Z, who are the two reasons Liberty gave up her dream of being a foster mom. When their lives were threatened, that's when that last line was drawn.

"Yes." Liberty went on to explain to her, "At the one black line, we saw something big had to be done. Everything had to end. And from there the end of the story is unknown. All that is left is hope for what we don't have any control over and—" she said, giving Mimi a little tighter hug, "our prayers for a very special little boy."

At this point Z started crying. "It's too sad! I don't want to talk about that quilt."

Obviously Liberty's heart came through her hands enough that even her kids felt it when they were looking at this big

Detail of Liberty Worth's *Timeline Quilt*

beautiful piece of painful art that somehow released pain stitch by stitch and tear by tear.

As for that white on the end, I'm drawn back to the book of Romans and the promise that "hope does not disappoint us, because God's love has been poured into our hearts through the Holy Spirit which has been given to us" (Romans 5:5, NRSV). That was a sustaining verse for me during my teen daughter's pregnancy, and it kept me believing in a good outcome even in trying circumstances. In many of the stories in this book, Spirit is obviously present when quilters need strengthening. Ironically a devastating part of Liberty's grieving was that God seemed so silent during her deepest despair. Admittedly she was angry with God. She and Jay had undertaken fostering with intentions of adopting as a way of serving God, so why didn't God protect them? They had the heart for it, but they'd never imagined getting chewed up and spit out like this. Where was God when the biological mother's mental state made Liberty and Jay afraid for the children's safety? And why was grief recovery taking so long?

Fortunately God can take rants and raves. Indeed, authenticity means being real. And Christians are assured that nothing can separate us from God, not even evil, loss, anger, or grief. The process of making the *Timeline Quilt* afforded Liberty the time, space, quiet, and focus she needed. Through the discharging experience of its making and slowly afterward, her grief became more manageable. She still believes in a God who loves her, and that's reason enough to let her sadness have its rest, to put off her heavy blanket of sadness, and to make room for joy, as Spirit whispered to her one morning. She feels like a tree that lost a huge limb in a storm. That loss threatened her stability, but she's learned to stand. She's grown deeper roots. She can't offer others the shade and protection she offered before, but she still has some shade and a little protection to spare.

* * *

Timeline Quilt was exhibited at the Glendale Quilt Show alongside a placard that said the quilt documented a family time that began with struggle and ended with hope. Liberty stood near the quilt for only a few minutes when she realized that it looked to others like any other quilt in the show. Onlookers wanted to know about the techniques she used, not about the story. Having it in this book is a different way of sharing it—presented along with the saga and Liberty's reflections on what happened.

In 2013, Liberty started making quilts on commission for clients and for textile companies needing samples using their new fabric lines, so now she gets to quilt from home, which provides some healing therapy (as quilting does for so many of us) plus an at-home income. More importantly, the Worths have learned that G, as he approaches his third birthday, is safe with a wonderful permanent family that also loves him. Liberty, Jay, Mimi, and Z are open to possibilities and hope again.

In retrospect, Liberty told me, she realizes that there's little in life that we can control or complete, but she finds the satisfaction of both control and completion in quilting. Certainly in fostering, they'd experienced the lack of control big time. Most of us know that family and kids are never *done*. Even with a painting, an artist may wonder when to stop or add something else. The quilter controls her design, colors, fabrics, placement, size and format, and the way the piece will be quilted, and in the end, as she takes the final stitches on the binding or facing, she knows her work is finished—her work on that quilt, that is. Our inner work continues day by day.

And indeed hope reigns! Just as this book was going to press, Liberty and her family were invited to be witnesses and felt honored and excited to be in court on the day of G's adoption by the wonderful family who will protect and love him forever. Although they miss G, they

Chris Boersma Smith

were overflowing with joy to see him and know he's in a loving and stable home. They rejoice in knowing that their sacrifice and pain, though deep, led this newly assembled family to have the wondrous delight they now have.

And not only that! Look at this picture of Liberty. A baby boy is expected in June 2014!

--- STEPS ALONG A SPIRITUAL QUILTMAKING PATH ---

CONSIDER HOW THE MODERN QUILT MOVEMENT MIGHT CONTRIBUTE TO YOUR STYLE.
The LA Modern Quilt Guild (LAMWF) was formed in 2009. Since then hundreds of other local chapters of the Modern Quilt Guild have started. With extensive online support and a lot of young moms and crafters as members, these guilds have a reputation for having younger members than the longer established guilds, although Liberty says the LAMQG is more diverse in age than the press might suggest.

Quilts featured within the Modern Quilt movement tend to feature minimalism, high contrast, graphic areas of solid fabric, and a bold color sense, but one would be hard-pressed to draw definitive lines between traditional quilts, art quilts, and modern quilts. All of those might involve updating of classic quilt designs, as well as extensive use of negative space and solids. In the early days of the movement, *Martha Stewart Living* featured Denyse Schmidt and called her quilts a "chic, modernist aesthetic," which spurred on the movement. Other Modern Quilt growth factors include the general public's burgeoning interest in design, digital cameras, and social media.

SMALL STEPS:
- Browse the websites of the Modern Quilt Guild as well as your local or even distant MQG chapters. Follow links to the teachers invited to address MQG membership.
- Note how the modern quilts you see compare to your own style and see if there are any elements of design you'd like to try either as part of a modern quilt or just to add something different to your own quilting style. Vice versa, if you're a modern quilter.
- Consider subscribing to an MQG online, attending a local meeting, or joining an MQG.
- You might also buy a book by a modern quilt author such as Denyse Schmidt, Alissa Haight Carlton (a founder of LAMQG), or Bill Kerr and Weeks Ringle. If you already have such a book or pattern, maybe it's time for you to make a modern quilt.
- If you're involved with a traditional quilt guild, how about inviting modern quilters to lecture or teach for your upcoming programs?

CONSIDER: SOMETIMES WE WORK DIFFERENTLY WHEN SPIRIT IS AT WORK. With her Timeline Quilt, Liberty broke from her typical approach. She machine quilts 85 percent of her quilts, and this one she hand quilted with perle cotton. Darra cut away a rectangle and made an arch she hadn't pre-planned.

ASK & JOURNAL: Review your own work and see if any quilts stand out as atypical in your creative process. Was there a particular reason that you diverged into a different approach, and if so, what? Was it logical or technical? Or was there perhaps a heart or Spirit-led reason?

SHARE: I'd love to have more modern quilters email chris.reapasyousew@gmail.com or submit a guest blog post about what you've experience regarding the connection between your textile art or crafts and your spirituality.

Earth-Spirit Emissary Wheel: We Saw the Light

Skeptics and left-brain-dominant thinkers will deny that auras exist. Or they'll explain them based on the physics of electromagnetic fields. But, for the eight quilting students crowded around a laptop one fall morning during a quilting retreat at my Bay Area home, the response to seeing a quilt with an aura was stunned amazement. Hollis Chatelain had just opened her e-mail to a picture of her friend Jane Stein's *Earth-Spirit Emissary Wheel* quilt. Jane had shared the photo that day for no conscious reason except that she felt prompted to do so. She'd finished the quilt about a month earlier.

As we stared at the digitally captured emanation of white light above and around the quilt, every one of this voluble group fell absolutely silent. I knew that I'd have to talk to Jane.

In our largely secular society few who've experienced a mystical tie between creativity and spirituality mention it openly out of fear of being judged as weird. Many of us may wistfully imagine how great it would be if the connection were obvious. Amazingly here was a visible springboard for conversations about how spirituality and quiltmaking connect.

Jane's Quilt Changed the Dynamics of the Group Who Saw Its Photo

After we saw the photo of Jane's quilt, we did more talking than stitching. Some accepted the quilt's aura as a spiritual manifestation, while the others at least entertained various possibilities. The women at my house had been gathering for annual workshops with Hollis for years. We were artistically bonded, and we'd shared many intimate details of our lives. However, we were diverse in many ways, certainly when it came to spirituality. Two of us were active in dream groups and Enneagram studies and had talked about that. Half had acknowledged having regular spiritual experiences. I believe I was the only one actively involved in an organized religion. Hollis knew that decades ago I took a class on paranormal psychology and learned to see auras. When she told our group that, I was suddenly less the oddball.

Our discussions about the connection between spirituality and quiltmaking went from admitting we had spiritual experiences to actually sharing what they were and how they how might relate to our quilting. One woman shared how she made a quilt representing her struggle to decide whether to quit an unfulfilling job and how that dovetailed with her enrollment in *A Course in Miracles.*™ Some mornings would begin with someone reading an inspirational passage she'd come across in her reading the night before. Hollis shared her spiritual experiences more explicitly. We moved beyond critiquing our work primarily from a design standpoint and became fascinated with what our creative choices reflected about our inner

Copyright 2008 by Jane Shaw Stein, *Earth-Spirit Emissary Wheel* (72"diameter), commissioned by Sancta Divina

workings. One woman admitted that quiltmaking no longer captivated her but said that photography did. As a group, we encouraged her to honor that, and we fashioned a way for her to stay with our group, even though she'd work on photography while the rest would continue to work on textile art. In short, the aura transformed our group.

Auras Have Been Depicted in Art for Centuries

Jane Shaw Stein lives in North Carolina, so after the retreat, I got permission to contact Jane and sent her an e-mail describing this book in progress. I asked for a phone interview and concluded by saying, "I hope you will say yes!"

Jane replied with an emphatic *YES!*

Before I interviewed her, I did some research about her and about auras, learning that for thousands of centuries artists have depicted people and gods surrounded by halos and auras of various sizes, shapes, and colors. Although representations of light and holiness around Jesus and Christian saints are familiar to most, few realize that fields of light were painted and carved around rulers, deities, spiritual teachers, and even cave men long before they appeared around Greek and Roman gods. Sometimes the light extended outward in shapes, thick rays, or thin lines representing a shining radiance. (Let's say *halo* when light or a disc surrounds the head only and *aura* when larger fields of light surround portions of their bodies as well.) Today we can easily find Internet images of many religions' deities and holy ones sporting halos or auras.

A number of people today are able to observe similar fields of light around people or objects. Today's aura observers tend not to attribute all the halos and auras in art to symbolism as some religious scholars do. Rather, it seems natural to them to assume that halos and auras appeared over centuries in many cultures' art simply because people saw them. Whether perceived with the naked eye or through what's known in some spiritual traditions as the third eye, the color and shape of auras are said to provide the observer with etheric, mental, or emotional information about the subject.

And etheric, mental, and emotional information is something Jane is very practiced at picking up!

Jane Is a Healer and Spiritual Peacemaker

For more than twenty years Jane has used touch, intuition, spiritual promptings, and loving presence to help others heal. She studied psychology and earned a master of science degree in special education with a concentration in autism. After a dozen years of working with special-needs youngsters, she moved into bodywork, first becoming certified in massage and later founding her current bodywork practice, Conscious Touch, in which she uses the Rosen Method™ (www.rosenmethod.org/) in a gentle, nondirective, nonjudgmental way.

She explained some principles of bodywork this way: Our bodies hold our emotional wounds as tensions until we're ready to identify and process them. Ignored, they stay with us as chronic reminders. Perhaps we've donned false selves because we've inhabited unsafe places, maybe because critical parent tapes continuously play in our heads, or possibly because we hear, absorb, and follow too many shoulds. Eventually in our quest to be real, we need to find where we carry our wear and tear. Through soft touch and keen observation, the Rosen practitioner notices where emotionally unmanageable experiences are recorded in the body.

Jane helps clients access the unconscious where wounds are buried. Once clients are more aware of root causes, they open up, and physical and emotional barriers may begin to dissolve. Jane said this practice is hard to describe verbally. It's only truly understood through experience. So true. Compare a description of how to ride a bicycle with actually getting on, pedaling, balancing, and steering all at the same time.

A year later on a Reap As You Sew retreat in Mexico, we saw this for ourselves. Jane offered everyone a Rosen session. For each of us the experience was unique and profound. For example, an unhealed foot that I'd neglected led me to acknowledge a lifelong issue of feeling there wasn't enough time to take care of myself or for people to listen to me. By the end of the long session as my breathing changed, I became more conscious of a time when others did listen to me, when I felt safe being my true self, flaws and all. I was completely intrigued when I realized that the day before I'd been Spirit-led to paint and stitch an abstract quilt (Sue Friedland style) that epitomized this very discovery. Buried inside some scrunched-up silk, I'd painted the names of all the people who'd listened to and accepted me as I was, and I'd allowed the quilt to have loose threads, irregular edges, and lumps.

Copyright 2010 by Chris Boersma Smith, *Accepted As I Am* (41" x 21")

Reiterating her belief in the inadequacy of words to convey meaning completely, Jane explained, "Without words you can effectively get through to the emotive level. That's why I also try to touch others' psyches or souls nonverbally through my artistic endeavors."

Jane Always Disliked the Exclusivity She Saw in Organized Religions

Most of her life Jane had an aversion to organized religions but an openness to spirituality. In church, sacred music sometimes resonated deeply in her, opening her to a sense of the divine. Yet she was always uncomfortable when followers expressed a we-they mentality, believing their way to be the only way. To her, this rejection of diverse approaches to God-consciousness diametrically opposes the universal spiritual truths conveyed by scriptures and the great teachers.

Encouraging inclusivity, Franciscan spiritual writer Richard Rohr put it in a way with which I think Jane would agree: Whether for healing or a meal together, Jesus never turned anyone away because of occupation, ethnicity, moral unworthiness, religious affiliation, or lack thereof, so he was basically showing us that God is everywhere, and therefore, God is not anywhere exclusively (*The Naked Now: Learning to See as the Mystics See* (Crossroad, 2009). The only ones Jesus didn't embrace appear to have been religious hypocrites.

In 1986, the leaders of the world's twelve major religions met in Assisi, Italy, the home of St. Francis, the mystical friar who loved all creation, generally acknowledged as the writer of the well-known beatitudes lyrics beginning, "Make me a channel of your peace." In Assisi the religious leaders offered prayers of peace from each of their traditions.

In 1994 a musician with a spiritual calling, James Twyman, took those prayers and in less than two hours arranged them to music "as if the music was already there, floating in space waiting for someone to catch them," he says on his website, www.emissaryoflight.com. Believing he'd been given an amazing gift to share with the world, he began presenting the sung peace prayers around the world, especially in countries beset by conflict. He founded (and still heads) The Beloved Community, an interreligious organization that has ordained more than five hundred ministers of peace.

Jane went to a Twyman concert, heard the peace prayers, and began visiting The Beloved Community's website. The site offers courses and forums. On one website visit Jane saw the announcement of a new Seminary of Spiritual Peacemaking master's program "to enhance the personal journey toward your 'Sacred Self.'" She was drawn to these words from lesson 1 in Twyman's *The Art of Spiritual Peacemaking* (Findhorn Press, 2016, containing lessons said to be inner teachings Jesus offered to his closest disciples 2,000 years ago) : "You have tried to hold still, but the days of waiting are now behind you. Are you ready to accept your mission …? Are you ready to bring peace to all beings by BEING peace? Say YES!" When Jane saw it, she realized that the act of saying *yes* was a serious commitment. The lesson also contained a word she'd rejected—*church*. Even so, the attraction of a seminary teaching spiritual peacemaking started to tug at her.

Jane resisted the calling until a month later when she heard a conversation in which a church member excluded a newcomer from the congregation's tight knit community. Back home afterward, Jane buried her head in her arms and cried at how belief systems supposedly centered on ideas of universal love, peace, oneness, and enlightenment are often lived in ways that spawn incredible divisiveness. Looking up after her cry, the natural world of her own beautiful yard with her cherished horses, roaming deer, and free-flying birds gave her a St. Francis moment. Suddenly she knew that she could be part of the solution, accepting all people as they truly are rather than sitting there and lamenting that religion as practiced is often so far from its stated ideals. She walked right into her house, went to her computer, and sent The Beloved Community her yes.

Two years later she was ordained, and today she's not only serving as a minister but also helping other students through their seminary experiences. Her goal is to allow room for all ways of finding God, Spirit, our higher selves, and elemental truth.

Oddly, when I e-mailed Jane about interviewing her, I'd also asked her to say yes. I'd never used that wording with anyone else. I just wrote to Jane as the Spirit moved me. My wording had special meaning for Jane, and her story of yes affirmed that we were meant to connect. Indeed, the very day we spoke on the phone, Jane picked up her lesson for the day in *The Art of Spiritual Peacemaking* (day 19), and it exhorted her to offer her gift to others, to extend her knowing to others, by—you guessed it—saying yes.

Jane's Emissary Quilts Are Based on Sacred Geometry

When asked about the making, the meaning, and the photography of the quilt with the aura, Jane told me it's one of an emissary wheel series, each done on commission. Jane created the first one, *Sacred Heart Emissary Wheel*, with hand appliquéd heavy satins. Technically not a quilt because it doesn't have three layers—it has no batting between the top and bottom—the piece was for a coach in the seminary, and it's now used in ordinations.

Copyright 2007 by Jane Shaw Stein, *Sacred Heart Emissary Wheel*, commissioned by S. Williams. For her first emissary wheel, Jane used reverse appliqué, sewing one fabric by hand on top of another and cutting away the excess to create the wheel.

The first piece triggered other requests for her to make more emissary wheels, including *Earth-Spirit Emissary Wheel*, which was a commission for Sancta

Chris Boersma Smith

Divina, a Wisconsin-based global community intent on bringing the divine feminine into the world.

In her quilting commissions as with her bodywork, Jane feels that acting intuitively or with spiritual guidance provides her with exactly what will resonate with her clients. Before going fabric shopping, Jane meditated with the woman who commissioned the quilt. They didn't discuss colors or fabrics. At the store a batik for the back and two fabrics for the front captured Jane's fancy—green batiks, an earth element like a forest floor (abstract, fertile, and feminine), and a light, subtle spiral on a soft multicolor background. When she sent photos of the fabrics to the client, the woman exclaimed that they were exactly what she'd envisioned.

Jane says that her spiritual calling is a ministry of the moment and that her creativity is part of that calling. She believes she creates what is here to be created now. Tending toward introversion, Jane likes to work by herself in her studio, where she looks out on her horses and natural surroundings. Yet her intention is outwardly focused—to have some impact in the world—without consciously planning just how to do so.

Alone in her studio, she prayed with every stitch she took on *Earth-Spirit Emissary Wheel*. She felt grateful and privileged to have the quilt commission. She tuned in to the hums and clicks of her sewing machine. She felt the project transcending herself and her client.

"Sacred geometry underlies each of the emissary wheel quilts," Jane told me. What is sacred geometry? It's a mathematical science—at least 2,500 years old—recognizing naturally occurring patterns and shapes. For example, crystals, snowflakes, oxygen, and DNA are said to share the same geometric structure. Plato promulgated the idea that everything in the physical world is based on five perfect 3-D forms composed of triangles (the Platonic solids). Modern scholars ridiculed the concept until the 1980s, when a University of Chicago physics professor developed a model showing that the pattern of the neutrons and protons in the nucleus of each element in the periodic table is based on

Earth-Spirit Emissary Wheel, photographed next to Jane's horses

the same five Platonic solids. (Robert J. Gilbert, www.shiftinaction.com/node/4423, June 2006). The golden ratio came out of sacred geometry and has governed the proportions not only of religious art but also of architecture ranging from pyramids to temples and cathedrals. More than a century before Plato, Pythagoras discovered the relationship between geometry and classical harmonics. The *sacred* tag derives from a respect for the geometry and ratios as part of a complex mystery, sometimes contemplated as the wisdom of the universe (Oliver Markley, *www.sacred-geometry.com/Sacred-Geometry/sacredgeometry.html*, April 8, 2010 and Paul Calter, *www.dartmouth.edu/~matc/math5.geometry/unit5/unit5.html*; April 8, 2010.)

"Since sacred geometry shows up in music, light, and the cosmos," Jane explained, "it connects with us, speaking on levels beyond the logical brain. Sacred geometry draws us in and triggers understanding through experience," she says.

Reap As You Sew

Copyright 2009 by Jane Shaw Stein, *Beloved's Emissary Wheel*, at Duke Gardens

"Quilters use it all the time. Stars, spirals, and circles are all elementary sacred geometry. We use it and respond to it, sometimes unconsciously, but it speaks to us on some level."

The emissary wheel is a sacred geometric symbol used in spiritual peacemaking as a path to personal and global enlightenment. It's got one center circle and twelve outer points, each point having a related word or attribute. Twyman brought the symbol to The Beloved Community after his experience with a group of people he called emissaries because they were messengers of peace who'd been using the wheel for generations as a form of divine connection and transformation. The wheel is used for meditation, and users are taught to reflect upon the points to assist in the path of awakening. The center represents stillness and the divine connection present within all living beings, according to Nikita Gearing, who published "Beloved World: Emissary Wheel" in 2007 on www.belovedworld.org.

Jane's *Earth-Spirit Emissary Wheel* is meant to convey the harmony and unity of "the twelve around the one," an archetype of mystery and truth. Jane also told me that spirals (like a nautilus) often have twelve elements around the center. Immediately I thought of Jesus and the twelve apostles, Yahweh and the twelve tribes of Israel, and Revelation's New Jerusalem with its twelve gates and twelve angels.

With its strong connecting lines, its center triangle and circle, and the peaceful blue-green contrasting with the pale swirly multicolor that reads almost white, Jane's quilt conveys a feeling that all is well, connected, and energetic yet calm. And that resonates with the twelve major religions' peace prayers and their being prayed together for one unified intention.

The symbols and the geometry inspired Jane, though she emphasizes that sacred geometry is not limited to one meaning because it speaks on levels that are beyond language. Still, as she worked, she focused on each point representing a different attribute—courage, patience, wisdom, certainty, compassion, joy, clarity, understanding, depth, generosity, abundance, and agape love (attributes James Twyman describes in his book). To Jane the equilateral triangle represents surrender, trust, and gratitude, and the circle, the stillness that is, the I Am. "But it's more about each one moving to her own center," she says.

Spontaneous as she is, Jane doesn't approach her creative work methodically or with a schedule, so she didn't set goals or deadlines for this commission. Indeed, whenever she would say, "I need to work on this now," she felt blocked. Only when *expansiveness* was present did a prayerful atmosphere allow her to create, bringing forth the wheel in what she calls its own divine timing. Because the woman who commissioned the work was a coach in the seminary, she understood that approach, and the six-month gestation was fine with her.

Indeed, when Jane finally shipped *Earth-Spirit Emissary Wheel*, it arrived at Sancta Divina just in time for their first anniversary celebration. Perfect timing!

Jane's Farewell Ritual Leads to the Surprising Aura

Jane always takes pictures of her completed quilts, usually indoors. With its earth-spirit and divine feminine commission, Jane felt that *Earth-Spirit Emissary Wheel* embodied an aspect of Native

American spirituality, which is always closely tied to the earth. Also knowing the quilt would be used in outdoor ceremonies, Jane felt led to go outside with her quilt and her digital camera. Her only thinking was that it would be best to put the quilt down where it wanted to be. She stopped at several spots around her three-acre property, but then she felt drawn to lay it on a clearing in front of her paddock.

In her words, "The farewell unfurled replete with gifts from the wheel itself and the spirit in which it was created." She'd be letting the quilt go out into the world to be used as Sancta Divina willed. She experienced her oneness with the quilt, acknowledged the creative energy that went into it, and bid it goodbye. And then she started shooting photos.

She was only aiming to document the quilt. Like most of us now that we don't have to pay for film and developing, Jane took thirty or forty shots in this spot and in others. When she downloaded the images, it was that first shot in the first clearing in front of the horses that showed the aura, the light emanating from the quilt.

Because Jane is used to evidence of greater possibilities and consciousness, she wasn't surprised to see the light. Rather, she felt joy, gratitude, and a strong sense that the quilt would serve some as yet unrevealed special purpose.

About a month later she e-mailed a copy of the photo to Hollis. She calls this an "unconscious inclusion" because she had no plans for the picture and simply shared it when it felt right. Neither she nor I cared whether the one photo with the light was a fluke because it just took one such photo to make our connection occur. The timing, which led Hollis to show it to my group and me to call Jane and ask to share her story with others, is music beyond our orchestrating. We never would've conceived the harmonies that would play out for each of us because of the thirty-day delay between Jane's photographing of the quilt and her attaching it to an e-mail to Hollis during the one week a year that Hollis was staying at my house. By the time of our interview Jane already saw that the aura photo and my inclusion of her story in this book evidenced Spirit moving as it wills to accomplish divine purposes.

Jane likes Mahatma Gandhi's philosophy, "You must be the change you want to see in the world." "Be who you are rather than who you think you ought to be. Open your eyes to what's in front of you," she says.

Like Jane and everyone else, I ride the roller coaster of life, and I need to recognize whenever I stop living creatively. Interviewing Jane reminded me that as she quilts in the Spirit, I need to write in the Spirit, not as a reporter but as a woman of heart and soul being transformed as I go about the interviewing and the writing. Interviewing her reminded me to allow myself to notice my fears, listen to their messages, and learn from them and then to kick out the fear and choose to listen to the voice of trust instead. Some self-imposed deadlines had led me to angst. Jane's story reminded me that my lawyer mind on a mission is far removed from flowing in the moment, letting go of deadlines and structure, and allowing unfolding, the powerful mystery of living in the now, the type of being that allows space for loving presence.

I acknowledge the desires of my heart and hope you will acknowledge your heart's desires too. I pray that we all live the ministry of the moment. I hope to join together with all who may pick up this book in a deep sharing to say yes to crossing the next threshold out of old comfort zones into our sacred callings. Like each element of *Earth-Spirit Emissary Wheel*, we're all an integral part. And together we—and our quilts—can be light in this world.

Reap As You Sew

Jain Prayer for Peace - detail from Jane's 2009 quilt for Lemurian Beloved

--- STEPS ALONG A SPIRITUAL QUILTMAKING PATH ---

CONSIDER HOW SYMBOLS HOLD POWER THAT CAN STIMULATE US CONSCIOUSLY AND UNCONSCIOUSLY, particularly if they've been used over a long time in religion or in myths and fairy tales representing archetypes like the heroine, warrior, earth mother, redeemer, temptress, or child.

ACT: Select a symbol with special personal appeal and make it the focus of a quilt. Many traditional blocks are abstracts of symbols like Jacob's Ladder or Crown of Thorns. Or create your own large or small design, whether it is obviously the chosen symbol or abstractly reminiscent of it. As you create, observe your insights into the symbol's power and meaning for you and the impact it might have on others as it goes out into the world. Remember, if this suggestion seems at odds with your beliefs, skip it. Also please note that I'm not suggesting the symbol itself is something to worship or idolize, or to replace God or whatever it represents. For me, a symbol is more like a switch that turns on a light. But it isn't the light itself.

ASK & JOURNAL:
- Jane often talks about doing things intuitively, and she's obviously a very spiritually open person. What's the distinction between intuition and a prompting of Spirit? It's generally accepted that all human beings have intuition—the ability to understand something immediately, instinctively or without conscious reasoning. Could it also be that believers in God are sometimes divinely influenced or led to know or to do certain things that reflect the will of God or divine inspiration? In either case, it may feel like an inner knowing, either from the inner self or from the Spirit within. Do you experience both and if so, do intuition and spiritual promptings feel different to you?
- Annie often talks about the idea of right-brained versus left-brained approaches. The right brain is commonly associated with creativity and emotions, and the left brain with linear and analytical thought. Are you aware which side of the brain is dominant in you during certain activities? You may wish to journal about ways to engage or disengage one or the other to suit your mood or needs.

CONSIDER INSTITUTING A RITUAL OF BIDDING YOUR FINISHED QUILTS FAREWELL (OR EVALUATE YOUR EXISTING PRACTICE). Sometimes we're so happy to finish a project that we rush it out the door without savoring the moment of its completion.

SMALL STEPS TO TAKE UPON COMPLETING A QUILT:
- Name and label your piece.
- Spend time alone with the finished piece, acknowledging the creative energy that went into it. If you sensed Spirit's guidance or inspiration, feel and express your gratitude, perhaps in Morning Pages or in your art journal.
- Say goodbye if you will not keep the quilt.
- Perhaps sensing where to do so, take pictures of the whole quilt, some showing details, and some even showing the back and the label if you like.
- Document your quilt as suggested on page 9, perhaps including an artist's statement.

SHARE: I'd love to have you email chris@reapasyousew.com any other outstanding photos of quilts with spiritually amazing stories. You may even wish to write or record one of these stories to submit as a guest post for the Reap As You Sew blog.

The Challenge, Some Gifts, and Conclusions

In our Hollis Chatelain annual workshop a year after we saw the photo of Jane's quilt, each student selected two related dye-painted fabrics. Hollis instructed us to sandwich and quilt one by contrasting areas of calm with areas of tension and to quilt the other with a repeating theme. After a day and a half quilting on our two whole cloth quilts, we gathered around a design board for critiques.

"The next challenge," said Hollis, "is to use both pieces and add another fabric or two for the borders, but the borders can't just be slapped on around the perimeter. They must be there as a design element, integrated into the rest of the quilt. But first—your turn, Chris—put up your two pieces and tell us what you did."

"I started with a spiral that seemed like a galaxy. I began in the center with three colors that blended in to create areas of calm. I increased the size of my motif and used red, orange, and violet threads as I moved outward to create areas that are not so calm. I like this piece a lot." Turning my attention to the other piece on the design board, I continued. "Here, a picture of tangled fibers inspired my quilting lines. This was fun to free-motion quilt with curving swirls, very organic and flowing, and I changed thread colors frequently. I followed the dyes, but I don't like how lumpy everything is. Although I had fun with it, I'm really disappointed with the way it looks. I just don't know how to get it to lie flat."

Hollis had a yet unexpressed theory in mind, namely that the dye-painted fabrics we'd just quilted would reveal our core issues, challenging us to face our resistances and continue our journeys with more spiritual guidance. "How do these pieces relate to your life?" she probed, leaving aside the technicalities and cutting to the chase.

"Hmmm," I stalled. "I think the top one with the nautilus represents the world that's recently opened up for me on the Sonoma Coast. I feel so much calmer when I'm there by the ocean," I replied. "The one with all the bumpy imperfections, the one I don't like, where the strands are crossed and tangled, that represents this house in Orinda. So much here reminds me of all the complications we've lived through here."

Hollis didn't just accept what I said. "Well, you stitched the nautilus with a walking foot, didn't you? Seems like you were aiming for more control. I remember your picture of anger in our color workshop the year Brenna was 16 and pregnant. It had sharp red zigzags and angled lines just like you have here. And here I'm seeing red thread, the color of anger. Controlled anger." Someone in the group whispered a "Wow!" and heads nodded.

At first I held my ground and argued, "But look, my points are cut off, not pointed."

Chris Boersma Smith

"Do you have your color notebook?" Hollis asked. I opened it up. Sure enough, she was right. In the workshop four years earlier she'd called out a series of feeling words, and for each we had a minute to draw the first image that came to mind. My spiral of points and my old sketch of anger were uncanny look-alikes, and a few squared off points didn't undo the similarities.

Reluctantly I admitted, "Okay, so I'm somewhat angry about the Sea Ranch house. I thought we'd be spending lots of weekends together there. I thought the kids and our grandson would love to come up to the beach. But I'm mostly there alone. Not what I expected."

Hollis nodded and then asked how I was going to combine these into one quilt. When I moved one to overlap the other and folded under a few corners to indicate a rounding off, she shook her head. "No, you can't integrate a border like that. And you're too attached to that nautilus spiral. You have to cut each section into at least three pieces."

"I can certainly cut up the swirly spiral," I replied, "but not the other one. I spent a whole afternoon quilting it just the way I wanted it."

"Cut it up," she insisted, giving me the raised eyebrow look that says to stop protesting.

Not sure I could just start cutting, I took digital photos of the pieces and the background fabrics. I played with paper printouts the next day, and later I had multiples printed at full size. I cut and rearranged them for a week after the workshop ended. When I cut both squares apart and arranged the paper pieces intuitively on a background to meet the integrated borders challenge, the composition began to resemble a headless woman—a woman unable to speak. I could relate to that because I'd been withholding feelings I didn't think Toby would want to hear. A necklike curve went from the implied head to the heart space, where I'd intuitively placed a cut-out spiral. Gazing at it and seeking meaning, I saw that the heart center symbolized how I was going in circles because of my confused feelings about my home and family. When I told another quilter that I liked the composition of the large snakelike segment coming up from the lower left corner but wondered if the shape was too phallic, she asked what was going on in my sex life. Another wow. "Funny you should ask. Not much these days," I replied. Through the evolving quilt, it seemed Spirit was unearthing feelings I'd been ignoring.

Six months later I was finally raring to cut into the quilted sections and construct the finished piece. I'd named it *Dualism Deconstructed*, realizing it was about replacing dualistic thinking with both/and thinking. *I don't need to dislike Orinda and love Sea Ranch, to be angry or guilty or hold back my feelings about having two homes and choosing to spend some time in the one that refreshes my soul the most and to spend some time in the one where my husband is when he's not away on business.* I had and enjoyed both and was grateful.

Copyright 2010 by Chris Boersma Smith, *Dualism Deconstructed* (28" x 40"), exhibited at *Images 2011*, Lowell, MA, and *Sacred Threads Exhibition 2013*, Herndon, VA

Besides, there's a long God story about why and how we have the Sea Ranch house. Suffice to say, I'm so happy to have a God who handles the details for us! We're blessed with the house and have set about to use it as the giver of gifts instructs us to. One of my first friends to see the place asked if I was going to give the property a name. Without a moment's hesitation, I replied, "Abba's Gift." (Jesus' name for his heavenly father was Abba, the equivalent of *Daddy*.)

From the beginning we thought Abba's Gift was one room too small because it lacked a studio. As we began to add on a studio and a garage, we ran into unforeseen defects caused by mice, underground water, the lack of central heating, and years of inadequate maintenance. Our remodeling project ended up taking three and a half years. It became my all-consuming focus. Just as construction was drawing to a close, I threw out my back and ended up hospitalized with a two-month recuperation period in Orinda. During that forced rest I initially read lots of books and pondered the meaning and purpose of my life. I thought it had to do with quilting and spirituality, so I decided I would finish this book, assuming that doing so was in line with my calling.

Then I got an e-mail from a Christian woman highly recommended by a trusted mentor, and that e-mail said there's a way for us to get rid of every single hindrance in our lives. I was simultaneously curious and extremely dubious. But I figured, *What's to lose other than about twenty dollars for a book and some time to read it?* (See Ericka D. Jackson's *Beyond Fearless: How to Remove Every Hindrance From Your Life*, New Creations Publishing 2009.)

There was going to be a webinar to explain how to get rid of all the common hindrances—fear, procrastination, doubt, not feeling good enough, anxiety, depression, jealousy, competitiveness, and even sickness or infirmity. I dove headfirst into this book of promise and came upon the first muddy sinkhole. I'd have to work on forgiveness as a precursor to the promised freedom.

Of course, it wouldn't be the first attempt I'd made at forgiveness, but there was a difference here. The recommendation was to list every situation that was still nagging at my heart in any way, and there was a prayer in Jesus' name for releasing the ill feelings one by one. I made the list, and it took two single-spaced pages, one line per situation. The most troubling situations involved my daughter Brenna becoming pregnant in high school, people judging us as *bad parents* because she got pregnant and/or because we supported her choice to keep the baby, all sorts of stuff about the father of her child, and a slew of ensuing legal matters. We'd done so much for Brenna and our grandson, but she'd stopped speaking to me for reasons I didn't understand. She hadn't even communicated when I was confined to the hospital or recovering after my back procedure, and I felt resentful. Yes, I had some work to do! I started with the easier cases and worked my way up to the Brenna-related situations.

The bottom line is this: in doing the forgiveness work, I realized how Brenna would never have ignored my pain had I not hurt her really badly. She's caring and compassionate by nature! Suddenly in one solitary afternoon at home, Spirit helped me see the many ways I'd made her feel "not good enough" throughout her life (while I'd been trying to parent her well). Not only did I forgive her, her son's father, and myself, but I forgave every hurt I could remember. I also wrote (with Spirit practically dictating) a long and specific apology to Brenna.

I had such an important reason to call her (about a legal matter) that I knew she'd answer the phone, and as soon as we connected, I told her I'd realized I owed her an apology. I said I hoped to talk to her about it in person if she'd come over for Father's Day a couple of days later. She came. I spoke some of my apology and then gave her the detailed letter, slipped into a card for her twenty-sixth birthday, which we were also celebrating on Father's Day. After she read it, she placed a handpicked bouquet and a note at my desk. The note thanked me for what she said was the best birthday gift she'd ever received.

I proceeded in the weeks and months that followed to do other spiritual cleansing work, and I was cleansed of all sorts of previously troublesome habits, negative thinking, fears, doubts, worries, and bad attitudes. I've never been so free to be my authentic myself. I had new enthusiasm for the creative process, and I'm also getting results that please me, including the quilt on the cover, *Let Spirit Flow*. That quilt was entirely guided by Spirit from finding Native American hand-dyed pig leather right down to the final quilting stitches. It had a lesson in it too. In the position in which it's pictured on the cover, I thought it was upside down because we usually read from left to right in our culture and keep upper areas lighter than lower ones. But Spirit told me no because it blows where it will, and the direction in which we might be pointed is up to Spirit!

Within the next six months my quilts were accepted in Sacred Threads, Images, Pacific International Quilt Festival and a Studio Art Quilt Associates Color Wheel of Emotions Exhibit, traveling to nine US venues. This book got submitted to the publisher. I hosted and attended quilting retreats and finished a number of small quilts.

There'd been a yearlong rift between our daughters, and they reconciled. Each of them moved into a better living situation. Toby and I turned Abba's Gift into our main residence and downsized our Bay Area home from the former family-sized house in Orinda to a small apartment in San Francisco. We've enjoyed a renewal in our marriage with great fun and we're sharing a new level of intimacy in this phase of our lives together. We've spent quality time and holidays with Brenna and our grandson. Their legal issues were favorably resolved, and their lives are incredibly improved. The kids even threw us a special thirtieth anniversary, complete with a DVD full of hundreds of their favorite childhood memories.

I also completed training programs for certifications so I could help others as I've been helped. I can work with Christians who'd like to experience freedom through the spiritual cleansing method I experienced. I'm engaging more in the spiritual direction practice I was trained for years ago (although I like to call it spiritual companioning or coaching rather than spiritual direction, because a good spiritual director doesn't actually tell others what to do). I can work with clients (of any spiritual belief system) who'd like Kaizen-Muse Creativity Coaching. I've been thrilled to get glowing feedback and, more importantly, to observe satisfying growth for clients who've been touched and transformed through our work together. I'm grateful to the Holy Spirit who blessed and guided this work as well as to the clients who were willing to open their hearts.

My Conclusions about Quilting and Creativity Time Being Sacred and Each of Us Having a Creative Mission

I'm excited about these changes and about opportunities to serve in connection with what I now know is not only a calling but also my heart's desire. I have no doubt that quilting or creativity time is sacred time—good for the body, soul, and spirit. "There is an appointed time for everything ... A time to weep and a time to laugh ... A time to tear apart and a time to sew together" (Ecclesiastes 3: 1, 2, 7, NASB). So it looks to me like God urges us to "go for it," affirming that there's a noble place in our lives for quiltmaking. I will still guard my time, however, so I also have daily quiet with God and nature (my Mary time), time for sacred self-care (which includes play time with my dog), and relationship time with my family and friends.

I'm convinced that now can be a time of renewal for you too. I believe you're endowed with certain talents, and you show you care for your gifts when you recognize, honor, and use them. If humans are made in the image and likeness of God (Genesis 1:26) and God has no body, then it's not a physical resemblance. If God is love (1 John 4:8), the disposition to love must be in each creature made in God's image. But what else is the essence of God (or the divine source if you prefer)? If God is the Creator of the earth and everything visible and invisible (Isaiah 40:28) and we're made in the Creator's image and likeness, then our creativity is godlike. We could be called co-creators, especially when we tune into divine inspiration during creativity. For me, that's why creativity is to be celebrated, encouraged, and pursued with a holy passion.

Of course, it's not always a smooth, straight path. Some of what holds us back is beyond our control and produces overwhelming stress.

Other hindrances have made their way inside us as negative self-talk, poor habits regarding time management, unwarranted procrastination, or paralyzing perfectionism. Perhaps we might call such blocks the enemies of our creativity. Enough! I choose not to let them come between me and my creativity anymore!

Psalm 37 declares that delight in the Creator will bring us the desires of our heart as well as safety from our enemies. Running into roadblocks, detours, delays, and obstacles is typical, whether situational, seriously habitual, or temporarily devastating. As I see it, creativity can provide a way out or a way through. For me, living the creative life I was created to live—at the intersection of spirituality and creativity—overflows with blessings in all areas of my life, and the desires of my heart are being fulfilled on a regular basis.

I hope some of the stories, reflections, and action steps in this book have resonated with you and that you're committed to the creative journey to be fully and freely your co-creative self. Take some quiet Mary time to listen. *Just imagine what your life and your quiltmaking or other creative pursuits will look like when you're free to be your true self and to engage in creativity to your heart's content. Open yourself to Spirit, and let it flow!*

--- STEPS ALONG A SPIRITUAL QUILTMAKING PATH ---

CONSIDER HOW QUILTMAKING CAN BE THE VEHICLE THAT GETS YOU WHERE YOU WANT TO GO.
Hollis's textile art is a vehicle to influence social consciousness and prompt change in the larger world. Her teaching also blesses and inspires others. Donna's quilts express her wonder in the world's continual unfolding to each consciousness and the endless magic of living. Darra, Liberty, and Annie's quilting has helped them through loss into new phases of their lives. Similarly my quilting helped me through anxiety and marital stress and ushered in a beautifully healed relationship. My cover quilt, Let Spirit Flow, expresses the idea of creative people being spiritually guided, and it has allowed me to share that view with others. Sue's creative process blends her meditation and her art in a way that grounds her. For Jane, her quilting is an extension of her ministry of the present moment, and it contributes to spiritual peacemaking.

ASK & JOURNAL:
- Whatever beliefs you embrace about the intersection of creativity and spirituality, ask yourself over a period of time how you might express that in your art. Let the question simmer in your subconscious, and ask Spirit to inspire you with some responsive ideas. The answer or answers may not come in words. Be open to ideas, images, and nudging from within.
- Who are you? What brings you joy? Ask yourself deep questions like these. Sleep on them in a Question Keeper. Let them percolate. Journal about them, if you wish. And also ask yourself how you might express that in your art.

***

CONSIDER WHETHER THERE'S DARKNESS YOU'D LIKE REPLACED WITH LIGHT. A good spiritual cleansing is probably as important as a periodic physical detox. Explore any way of doing this that resonates with you or seek spiritual assistance.

***

SHARE: I'd love to have you email chris@reapasyousew.com with a proposed guest blog post, comments, personal experiences, or anything you'd like to discuss relating to the connections between spirituality and quiltmaking. I'd like to invite you to a forum where spiritual quilters can connect with each other with some privacy, so let me know if you're interested in that, too.

***

ACKNOWLEDGEMENT: I'd like to acknowledge that many of the STEPS ALONG A SPIRITUAL QUILTMAKING PATH were influenced by Jill Badonsky, the founder and creator (along with Robert Mauer, Ph.D.) of Kaizen-Muse Creativity Coaching™. Jill also wrote and illustrated some great books and other products on creativity, and she was my inspired Kaizen-Muse Creativity Coaching™ trainer. She did such a good job that I can no longer think or talk about creativity without her ideas permeating what I now have to say on the subject! Much of what I wrote *Before Jill*, I've since tweaked. I hope you find her influence as helpful to you as it's been for me and my fellow Kaizen-Muse Creativity coaches and our clients. She can be found at www.kaizenmusecreativitycoaching.com.

About the Author

A quilter for two decades, Chris Boersma Smith considers textile art her sacred passion. *Reap As You Sew* explores how quilting and spirituality work together for quilters of various spiritual beliefs, impacting the quilts' artistry as well as the quiltmakers' lives and the community. Chris believes creative pursuits can help every woman become the unique work of art she was created to be. She hopes this book will help quilters find new ways to pursue their creative passions with greater joy than ever.

Chris is active in quilt and art groups, including Christians in the Visual Arts, the International Association of Creative Arts Professionals, and Studio Art Quilt Associates. She has created over 125 quilts, ranging from traditional bed quilts to contemporary fiber art for the wall. Her quilts have won numerous awards and netted thousands of dollars for charity.

For ten years Chris has hosted intimate quilt retreats, and she cherishes the deep connections and breakthroughs that happen in that setting.

An avid student of theology, spirituality, and scripture, Chris is an alumna of Georgetown University and the Monastery of the Risen Christ School for Charismatic Spiritual Directors. She has served in a broad range of ministries. She's also a member of the Kaizen-Muse™ Certified Creativity Coaches Coalition, and the Kingdom Training Institute's Convergence™ Coaches' network.

Raised in the Midwest, Chris lives with her husband and their Cavalier King Charles Spaniel in a remote coastal community 110 miles north of San Francisco, not far from one of their daughters and their grandson in Sonoma County, California.

Website: www.ReapAsYouSew.com